Other books by Dr. Robert Sneider PsyD

SSTOP: School Shooter Threat Onset Predictive
The Pathology of Bullying, Violence in Schools and the School
Shooter Syndrome
Strategic Book Publishing and Rights Company
www.sbpra.com

Novels by Robyrt Snyder

The Wycked Falls: Descent into the Maelstrom
The Falls II: In the Crossfire of Mist and Madness

AMERICAN LYNCHPIN

THE SPIRIT OF FREEDOM AND THE SECOND CIVIL WAR

Dr. Robert Sneider PsyD

Order this book online at www.trafford.com
or email orders@trafford.com

Most Trafford titles are also available at major online book retailers.

© Copyright 2020 Dr. Robert Sneider PsyD.
All rights reserved. No part of this publication may be reproduced, stored in a
retrieval system, or transmitted, in any form or by any means, electronic, mechanical,
photocopying, recording, or otherwise, without the written prior permission of the author.

Scripture quotations marked KJV are from the Holy Bible, King James Version
(Authorized Version). First published in 1611. Quoted from the KJV Classic
Reference Bible, Copyright © 1983 by The Zondervan Corporation.

Print information available on the last page.

ISBN: 978-1-4907-9930-8 (sc)
ISBN: 978-1-4907-9931-5 (e)

Because of the dynamic nature of the Internet, any web addresses or links contained in
this book may have changed since publication and may no longer be valid. The views
expressed in this work are solely those of the author and do not necessarily reflect the
views of the publisher, and the publisher hereby disclaims any responsibility for them.

Any people depicted in stock imagery provided by Getty Images are models, and such
images are being used for illustrative purposes only.
Certain stock imagery © Getty Images.

Trafford rev. 03/06/2020

 www.trafford.com
North America & international
toll-free: 1 888 232 4444 (USA & Canada)
fax: 812 355 4082

CONTENTS

DEDICATION

To my beautiful wife and partner in crime, Simone, who has been by my side for every step of this literary adventure.

And to the American Spirit of Freedom and Exceptionalism.

INTRODUCTION

"FREEEEEEEEDOOOOOOOOM"

William Wallace, Scottish rebel with his last dying breath from the movie "Braveheart."

I hear the sound of something else. It sounds like a drumbeat in the distance.

It's coming closer.

It's the sound of marching. It's boots in the street. First hundreds, then thousands, then millions. I hear the sound of angry voices.

It's getting closer.

I hear wooden sticks and the clash of steel.

I hear the papers ripping and tearing.

I see the colors waving. I see the smoke. I hear the guns. I see the blood.

I wish it could stop.

I feel the pain, the rage and the hate.

I wish it could heal.

A single bell pierces the raging tumult. A single bell tolls in the darkness.

I hope it is the ring of freedom.

I fear it is the death knell of America.

It's coming.

Can you hear it? Can you see it? Can you feel it?

The current rendition of the Democratic Party is a party of contradictions. It is a party that is increasingly in disarray and is more and more evident that as the next election draws near it is a party of desperation. It started with the debates.

Kamala Harris and Cory Booker were low in polling numbers, couldn't qualify for some of the debates and then ran out of money and had to drop out. They claimed it was because of racism. But did they forget that only Democrats were involved in the process therefore, in effect they were calling their own party racists. I guess that happens when one is so used to applying that label every time anything runs contrary to a liberal viewpoint.

Beto O'Rourke proposed to tear down the wall at the southern border and to confiscate guns. He was gone soon after. I guess his claim of being "born to be president" was a birthright hatched in a bubble like so much of the liberal agenda. Tom Steyer, a never-Trumper, finances his way onto the debate stages and runs on an environmentalist platform. The only problem is that he made his money investing in fossil fuels. Elizabeth Warren claimed fake Indian status her whole life and has built a house of cards on a rotten foundation. As she lectures the rest of us on how immoral we are, the public sees through it and her campaign is tumbling down around her ears. Mike Bloomberg was tough on crime when he was mayor of NYC but had to apologize for his "Stop and Frisk" program or be accused of, what else, racism. He crystallized the elitist view that the left has of the rest of the country, when he disparaged farmers for not having enough "gray matter". He is another environmentalist who flies a private jet to Bermuda every weekend.

Then there is Bernie Sanders who has to worry about his own party sabotaging his election because they don't like him. Finally, there is the front-runner Joe Biden who said he will beat Trump like a drum in the general election but comes in 4th or 5th in his own party's primaries. People are supposed to get wiser with age but here is a man who has run-ins with the people who attend his rallies (not very many by the way). He called one woman supporter "a lying dog-faced pony soldier." Biden is an anomaly all unto his own and not because he doesn't know where he is most of the time. He might be the only politician in the history of the world whose strategy to win elections is to tell the voters NOT to vote for him. And then he appears absolutely stunned when the voters do exactly what he advises. Now that is a special kind of stupid.

But it gets worse. If Biden gets the Democratic nomination it will be engineered through a brokered convention and the orchestration of superdelegates. This is how the Democratic party rolls. The elites (never the people God forbid) decide what is best for the country and who should lead it. And they want to do the same thing to the rest of the country. Mark these words; if Biden is the nominee, he will just be a figurehead for the Democratic establishment and the strings will be pulled by the power brokers behind the scenes. This is something that is right in the bailiwick of the left. Where have we seen this before? We don't have to go very far.

For two years we watched an independent counsel who we all *assumed* had some integrity, conduct an investigation into alleged Russian collusion into the 2016 election, spending millions of taxpayer dollars in the process. Everyone waited with bated breath for the vaunted Mueller Report. However, it wasn't until Robert Mueller had to give testimony before Congress that he was exposed as the front man for the whole sham. It was evident as soon as he opened his mouth that he was incompetent, unknowledgeable about what was in his own report, biased, and frankly not in clear possession of his own mental faculties. It was apparent that he probably didn't have very much to do with conducting the investigation or writing the report because he was incapable. But that didn't stop the liberal powerbrokers. They propped him up like "Weekend at Bernie's" and used him to give *their* work the necessary credibility that a totally fake and biased report would need. And we watched the whole hoax crash and burn right before our eyes, quicker than the Hindenburg, the minute Mueller spoke.

The analogy with Biden is almost chilling. Once again, we will have the pleasure of watching an aged, incompetent, incomprehensible, spokesman with deteriorating mental faculties bumble and dodder his way through a rigged campaign as the front-man for the Democratic Party. Because frankly it is all they have left.

If you are confused by all of this, not to worry. So is everyone else. Welcome to Democrat party politics in 2020.

Meanwhile Donald Trump is sailing along with a prosperous economy, relative peace, keeping his promises and draining the swamp. Any other president in any other time would be elected automatically on this kind of record. But these are not ordinary times. Trump has wounded the Democrat Party and there is nothing more dangerous or unpredictable than a wounded animal. Case in point, Nancy Pelosi.

After the President's State of the Union, the country was stunned to watch Nancy Pelosi rip up her copy of the speech in front of the whole nation. It was an unprecedented act of disrespect. But even more important it was SYMBOLIC. It was a chilling metaphor for what is in store for our country. It was as if she was ripping up the country right down the middle and she wanted everyone to take note. Author Michael Snyder termed it a "harbinger". He is exactly right and it was predicted in this book, American Lynchpin.

It is just the beginning of what this country will be subjected to in the coming months and years. It is the modus operandi of the Left. They are sensing that their hope for winning the 2020 election is dwindling and they are readying their default strategies. The first of those is to create chaos among the American people. The second is a scorched earth policy of total destruction and nothing is off the table--not the constitution, not our values or institutions and not the well-being of our country. It is almost incomprehensible that these people are our fellow Americans but that is almost an obsolete concept in these times.

If you think we are not there yet consider this; which might serve as the epitome of the hatred of the left for the rest of us, (as if what has preceded this isn't chilling enough.) It's a little article that comes from Metro reporter Jimmy McCloskey who quotes Denver Democrat Councilwoman Candi CdeBaca, "For the record, if I do get coronavirus I'm attending every MAGA rally I can." Think of the magnitude of this. This is a woman in public service whose commitment to elected office should be the well-being of her fellow citizens and instead has promised to intentionally infect them with a serious disease that has sickened and killed thousands of men, women and children worldwide. This is what she, as an elected public servant of the American government wishes to inflict on her constituents and her fellow countrymen and her nation. They really do want to kill us.

Folks, from here on in, the road is about to get very rough and the American people better buckle up! There is a maelstrom brewing on the horizon.

Rockin' in the Free World by Neil Young
There's colors on the street
Red, white and blue
People shufflin' their feet
People sleeping in their shoes
But there's a warnin' sign
on the road ahead
There's a lot of people sayin'
we'd be better off dead
Don't feel like Satan
but I am to them
So I try to forget it
any way I can.
Keep on rockin' in the free world.

PART I

THE SPIRIT OF FREEDOM

Recently my wife and I undertook a journey across America by car. We jokingly referred to it as 30 days in a Prius, our version of Around the World in 80 Days. Neither one of us had ever attempted an endeavor of this nature before. It was truly transformational for the both of us.

Our takeaways from this adventure, were of how vast this country really is, even by modern metrics. Consider that at a time when this country was expanding westward, the principal mode of transportation was on foot or by horse and wagon--and the hardships were infinitely greater. An advance of ten miles per day was considered admirable progress

Today, we can cover as much ground, in a number of hours, as these pioneers were able to travel in a month. And even by our current standards of mobility, this country still represents an enormous amount of territory.

I think what struck me aside from its enormity, was the diversity. Geographically, this country is a phenomenon of nature, in which almost every physical formation imaginable, from mountains to deserts and everything in between, is represented.

Moreover, it is culturally diverse, as well. In many instances, the geographical differences dictated the cultural development. For instance, the grasslands of the plains led to the great herds of buffalo which gave rise to the nomadic Indian tribes, that based their very existence on the buffalo. They would eventually be supplanted by domestic herds of cattle and the great agricultural enterprises, of what would come to be known as the 'breadbasket' of America.

We saw vast disparities in wealth and how people lived, from a dusty mobile home, in Cody, Wyoming, to a 30-million-dollar mansion, bordering the Pebble Beach Golf Club. To be truthful, I was in awe of it all, but in the face of such extreme diversity, I was left with a question to ponder.

"What keeps it all together? What is the denominator, the common thread that somehow, unites us all?"

I surmised that it was something that reaches quite deep and far back because the disparate nature of our country didn't happen overnight. It has been there from the beginning.

After some retrospection, with some help from a previous career as a teacher and historian, I concluded that there was one element that has transcended all physical boundaries, ideologies, economic disparities and even time itself. And that was the 'spirit of freedom' (something that, sadly, is seldom taught in our schools anymore.)

This is a country that was founded on that spirit. "Conceived in liberty", was how Lincoln phrased it. It's in our blood. It's in our DNA.

Freedom of religion brought the first settlers to our shores and their God-based spirit of freedom is the very soul of our country. It was integral at the time of our inception, it has preserved this country through perilous times, and unfortunately, I fear, our spirit of freedom will be our downfall.

There is no doubt that we are a unique country; one that is exceptional in the history of the world, (something else that is no longer taught in our schools, but rather, the very opposite-that we should be apologists).

Up to the time of our declaration of independence and the beginning of the great American experiment, the civilizations and societies of the world were run by kings and dictators who derived their power from their bloodline, or by brute force. Once in power, they instituted systems that were designed to keep the masses of people (or subjects as they were known) under their submission and keep themselves in power.

The average peasant was not free to do as he or she pleased. He/she was subservient to the king and he/she did the king's bidding or faced consequences, some of which could be extremely dire, depending on the discretion of the king. The peasant was told what his/her role in life would be, and he/she had little choice in the matter.

This kind of authority would eventually evolve into caste systems and feudal systems and other hierarchies of labor and servitude, designed to perpetuate the power structure and keep control of the population from birth to death. The most determining factor, one that determined your fate in this kind of society, for the rest of your life was, who your parents were. It was as if you were a breed of dog.

Some regimes were more oppressive than others and ran the gamut from socialism to communism to slavery (sometimes it was hard to distinguish one from the other). Under any of these systems, few people were free to determine their own fate and there was no such thing as elections. That concept would be inconceivable to a medieval serf.

The discovery of America changed all that. It offered an interesting alternative to people who rejected the tyranny, of having to live a life in a system in which someone, with no other qualifications than their lineage, got to dictate how you were to live every aspect of your life.

People saw an opportunity to escape that kind of oppressive dominance, albeit, at great risk and peril to their own existence. There was a high likelihood that it might require you to pay the ultimate price. However, death is rarely a deterrent to someone imbued with the spirit of freedom, and that is a theme we will see repeatedly, throughout the course of this writing. In fact, it was the message stamped on the front and back of our car, that we carried with us to all the other states, that we visited on our recent excursion. It's a sentiment that everyone who lives and drives a car in New Hampshire sees, on a daily basis. Our license plates proudly proclaim it, "Live Free or Die" for anyone who cares to take note.

It honors how precious that sentiment was to those that risked their lives to come to these shores and how badly they craved freedom. It was their chance to be able to speak their own language, to be free to express themselves, to worship who and how they wanted and to conduct their life in a manner they deemed fit. "They" became the operative word. "They" would get to decide.

And so, America became "the great experiment" where the power, for the first time in the history of human civilization, was entrusted to the people ("of the people, by the people, for the people".) For the first time, it was "the people" who decided their own fate and it ran radically contrary to everything that had preceded it. No more kings! No more despots! There would be elections to determine the "will" of the people.

This is all very important because it goes to the heart of a country that was founded on these principles. If freedom is the soul of this country, the Constitution and the principles and institutions it embodies, are the heart of our country. A country, where a man is measured by his merits and judged by his accomplishments; not the color of his skin or who his parents were.

In fact, what mattered most was what an individual did and not who he was. *That*, is what made America unique and exceptional. We embraced this experiment based on the spirit of freedom, and while it has never been perfect, that spirit and the ingenuity and the entrepreneurship that it unleashed, made us the wealthiest, most powerful nation in the world.

One of my favorite movies is "Braveheart." I have always wondered why I was so fascinated with this film, and I surmise it is because it so embodies the spirit of freedom. The Scottish people fought and died, so that their country might be free of English rule. However, while that might have been important to the Scots it was not even close to the kind of freedom that America envisioned. On closer inspection, it is true, that the Scots would not have to contend with rule under an English monarch, but they would still be governed by the rule of a Scottish king. And while that might be *less* oppressive, it still didn't deliver any rights to the individual. In that sense, it was a poor intonation of the American brand of freedom.

American freedom is as exceptional as the country itself. Patrick Henry once expressed the essence of the Americanization of freedom in a few simple words, "Give me liberty or give me death." I don't know if this would have made it to a license plate even if there were cars back then. This was not exactly a benign proclamation when you consider that he was flaunting it in the face of the most powerful nation in the world, at the time. A rebel, if caught, was more than likely to be given the back end of that choice.

One of the most incredible stories that I have ever read was in Edward Burrows ground-breaking "Forgotten Patriots", that tells the horrendous story of the American prisoners who were captured by the British in the Revolutionary War. In the duration of that war, some 200,000 Americans fought against our British foes. Approximately 6,800 soldiers died in battle. What is incredible, is that it has been estimated, that as many as 32,000 American patriots may have been captured by British forces and that 11,000 to 16,000 may have died in captivity. If we accept the higher estimate, that is almost three times the number of men that died in actual battle.

During that time, American prisoners of war were generally brought to New York, by the British, who used that city as the base of their military operations in colonies. Once there, they were housed in whatever facilities were available, (usually old warehouses or sugar houses). However, when these spaces were filled, the British began employing old hulks of warships and anchoring them in Wallabout Bay.

The conditions in the holds of these ships, were some of the cruelest and most inhumane ever perpetrated on fellow human beings. Thousands of men would be crammed into spaces, that were only meant to accommodate a few hundred. Rations were rancid at best and unsustainable for anything but slow starvation at worst. The men below decks were covered in lice and human excrement. Disease was rampant and it decimated these prisoners, at the rate of 70% in some cases.

The part that is truly incomprehensible about this situation, is that if you took an oath to join the Loyalist movement, you were immediately released from these hellish dungeons. In some cases, you did not even have to swear allegiance to the crown, but just promise not to take up arms against the British if you were released. It was literally a decision that held life and death in the balance. Few prisoners took the British up on their offer and approximately 16,000 chose to die, for the freedom of their country.

> "So wedded were they to their principals, so dear to them was their country, so true were they to their honor, that rather than sacrifice them, they preferred the scoffs of their persecutors, the horrors of their dungeon, and in fact even death itself."

Edwin Burrows, "Forgotten Patriots"

> It was the ultimate example of what an American was willing to endure, in the name of freedom.

How inspirational, that, here was a country that had that kind of spirit of freedom incorporated into its cornerstones. How was it possible that a country, infused with such an endemic devotion to patriotism could ever *not* succeed?

And so, I wondered about that too. There have been many great civilizations of the world and the one thing they all have in common is that they all collapsed or disappeared. From the Greeks, Egyptians and Romans to the Mayas, Incas and Aztecs of the Americas, they all fell for one reason or another-whether it was attributed to internal strife or external forces of nature.

I am afraid that this same fate will befall this great American empire of ours, as well. My wife tells me that America does not play a role in Biblical end times prophecy. In fact, as hard as Biblical scholars try, the world's greatest superpower even by extension hardly garners a mention at all. Although no one knows exactly when this apocalypse will occur and seeing firsthand the greatness that we have achieved as a nation, it hardly seems possible that we could suffer such a precipitous decline.

But there is no denying that there are many precedents in the course of history.

And our cracks are beginning to show.

As recently as 10 years ago, I would have scoffed at such a suggestion and if such a calamity were to befall us, there would have been no doubt whatsoever, that it would have been something foisted on us from some outside entity or foreign incursion. But in the last 10 years, it has become far more conceivable, that our downfall will be of an internal genesis.

"We" are likely to be the cause of our own downfall.

To underscore this, it was the same thing that was foreseen by Lincoln before the Civil War.

> "America will never be destroyed from the outside.
> If we falter and lose our freedoms, it will be because we
> destroyed ourselves."

There are many who fear we are rotting from the inside out. And have been for awhile.

My fear is that the spirit of freedom, which was the source of our birth as a nation will also be the ultimate source of our demise.

New York senator Henry Seward called it an "irrepressible conflict."

Eight out of ten people polled say they believe that the country is "mainly" or "totally' divided.

NBC/WSJ survey 10/2018.

There is a growing sentiment, in the majority of people in America, who believe that given our current state of affairs, we have never been more divided as a country. It is not only a political rift but it seems to be generational and cultural. People are starting to realize that they have nothing in common with their fellow countrymen. There is no common ground for compromise. That is remarkable considering all the instances of polarizing events that have occurred in our past, such as civil rights, abortion and the Vietnam War, just to mention a few. However, none of those controversies were divisive enough, to actually split the country apart.

Nevertheless, there is a precedent that did exactly just that-- tore this country asunder; resulting in four bloody years of slaughter that had brothers killing each other. It was the ultimate schism. The American Civil War was unquestionably one of the darkest times in our nation's past.

The first Civil War is the blueprint for how a country becomes *so* divided, that it tries to annihilate itself. We must recognize it as such. We would be wise to study it, dissect it, deconstruct it and learn the lessons that it has to teach us, if we have any hope for the salvation of our country in the future.

We must take the words of Mary Chestnut to heart on the eve of the Civil War.

"We are divorced, North and South, because we have hated each other so."

We must regard her words as a harbinger.

The rest of this book is about how that is likely to happen. This book will examine scenarios of past and present, in order to elicit what is likely to happen in our future.

In actuality, I write this book in the hope that it will inform and educate its readers, who will then recognize the true nature of the issues that divide us, and work to avoid the consequences that face us, together as a nation. It is my sincere hope that this book might act as an agent of change and I pray to God, that we can find a way to live together in peace.

For nothing that has not already happened is written in stone.

And so it goes.

Robert Sneider, 12/27/2019.

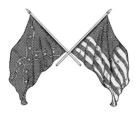

A CODICIL OF A PERSONAL NATURE

No book is written in a vacuum, no author without bias, and I feel that it is important that the reader have some information about the originations of a piece of writing, especially a work of this nature. The premise for this book was spawned fifteen years ago when I was an educator in the New York City school system, even though I did not know it at the time. More recently, it was triggered by travels to Gettysburg and Dallas and it will become evident to the reader, how each played a role in the writing of this book.

This work is a comparison of two different periods of time with an interpretation of events that occurred in the past and the present, from which this author extrapolates based on his education (psychologist, historian) experiences (life, travel and teaching) about what might occur in the future. This book is borne out of my interpretation and my opinion and so it is only my opinion when I proclaim that what will happen in the future is inevitable.

I'm just an average person. I don't claim to have any inside information and I do not possess any special powers of intuition or divination. Even though I have earned a doctorate, I do not regard this as a badge of intellect. I consider most of the knowledge I have acquired to be self-taught. I have had a life-long thirst for knowledge, and I am an avid reader.

What I do have, is the willingness to look at history and the ability to reason and to think critically. And I didn't even have to go to "The Wizard of Oz" for it, as did the scarecrow. Although I dare say, that if you want to acquire this skill nowadays, you probably will have to leave the country-- given the current state of education in America. Fortunately, it was a skill that I learned in grade school in Canada (at a time when such things were considered important requisites to getting an education) and one that has been an invaluable companion ever since.

It was a tool that enabled me to write this book because sometimes, it is impossible to have *all* the facts. And sometimes, you don't *need* all the details. Sometimes, all you need is the ability to reason and the wherewithal to fill in the blanks. Sometimes, all you need is logic to read between the lines. The writing of this book was one of those times when I relied on all those faculties, and why I feel like I got it right. When I was done, I felt like I had put a key into a lock, all the tumblers fell into the correct alignment slots and the door opened.

Sometimes, you just *know* when a thing is right.

I also have a confession to make.

I am a conservative.

I am proud to say I am a conservative-- this book is proof of that. But I have friends and family all over the political spectrum. I am in agreement with some more than others, although I am sure I have had disagreements with all of them at some point. Through it all we have remained friends. It is because despite being of different points of view, we respected each other's integrity as people.

I have been a conservative during all those friendships. I was raised as a conservative from a young age and have been one all of my life. I can hear all the clicks on my Facebook account now, unfriending me as I speak. That's okay. I understand. After working the last 15 years in 'liberal-land', it's not a surprise. I'm used to it by now. I get it. It's the world we live in.

In the past, if one wanted to keep their political affiliations to themselves, they just had to refrain from talking about politics, but it is not so easy these days. Politics are infused into the culture. Political parties are no longer something that you vote for. Now, they operate under the auspices of the culture they represent. Today you don't vote for a party you *are* the party and the party is the culture. Nowadays, you can talk about any number of everyday subjects and if you speak for any length of time people will be able to determine your political bias. Take immigration, for example; one side is for open borders, the other is not. Depending on which side of the issue you happen to support, you are either compassionate or a racist. Do you see what I mean? The only way you can go undetected these days, is to not speak at all about anything. I don't know many people today who are willing to do that—in fact, it is quite the opposite—people are more than willing to rant infinitum. And ad nauseum, I might add. But since you were going to find that out anyway (my bias), in the normal course of our conversation (this book), I felt that it was my responsibility to give it to you straight. I am a conservative.

It's who I am.

I can no more deny who I am as a person than a fish could swim out of water.

But wait. I have more shocking news to report.

I once met Donald Trump at a rally and I donated money to him and I worked for his campaign in 2016 and I voted for him as president.

I know—click, click, click.

But I never shook his hand. That was on purpose. After 4 years of seeing what Obama was doing to our country, it was evident to me that he was taking us in the wrong direction. I began to get more involved in politics. In previous campaign rallies I had shaken the hands of Mitt Romney, Ted Cruz and Rick Perry and they had all lost. I didn't want to jinx another Republican candidate.

In fact, I still have a "Drain the Swamp" poster from the 2016 election. Who knew at the time, it would prove to be so prophetic?

Uh oh, more clicks, less friends.

I guess unfortunately that is the climate we live in today and it is the story of two Americas. It is where we are as a country as I write this in 2019. In case you are a liberal and believe that Donald Trump is the sole reason for our country being so divided, I urge you to read on as well, because having a vested interest in the welfare of our country should not be a partisan concern.

So yes, I am a conservative and that is who I am. I will not deny it and I will not apologize for it. In fact, I have earned the right to be called a conservative because I paid my dues in a host of less-than-friendly environments. There were many times in my career where I had to act like I was apolitical in order to continue drawing a paycheck, specifically in the heavily liberal, dominated education environment of New York City. I was not always successful in that endeavor.

But before we get to that, there is the issue of branding. This isn't the first time, we conservatives have been derogatorily labelled, from Hillary Clinton's "basket of deplorables" to Peter Strzok's "smelly Walmart shoppers" to individuals who "cling to their guns or religion" as Barack Obama said. I shop at Walmart; guilty. I am a deplorable; guilty. I cling to God, guns and my Bible; guilty. I live in a small town; guilty. And I believe in "the Ghost in the sky" and the "Noah and the Ark fairytale". That is OK. I am not going to melt like a snowflake or crack like an egg.

As I discussed in a previous book, "SSTOP: School Shooter Threat Onset Predictive", a book about what makes school shooters tick--something we will delve into a little bit later in this book, there was an old adage in the time when I was growing up that went something like this; "sticks and stones will break my bones but names will never hurt me."

Calling a true conservative, names, is not going to make them abandon their principles. At least, I would hope that would not be the case because then you have what is known as that most slimy infamous creature that slinks through the political swamp; the notorious RINO (Republican In Name Only). Or if you prefer, Pierre Delecto aka Mitt Romney.

And while I think this tactic of name calling is not personally offensive, I think mischaracterizing one half of the country who supported Trump is a huge miscalculation by liberals. If you malign half the country, you are now setting up a dangerous dynamic that will result in the escalation of rhetoric, physical violence and ultimately civil unrest. If the left wants to criticize Donald Trump for his style on an individual basis, I think these leftists would find some common ground on that point with Republicans and conservatives. As a conservative, I support most of the actions and policies that President Trump has enacted, because I believe that America, as a country, is benefiting from the results.

But I will admit that sometimes his personal behavior makes me cringe, however I understand he is a fighter, something that Republicans have been lacking for a long time and I would rather have a president who loves this country, puts America first and gets results; even though he is a little rough around the edges, than a president who speaks eloquently, as he constantly lectures us about what is politically correct and gets nothing done.

That's what we had for the *last* eight years, before Trump. And that is my right to criticize Obama, (without being called a racist) just like it is the right of a liberal to criticize Trump.

I think that Hillary Clinton underestimated the effect of calling the right a "basket of deplorables" and that it hurt her campaign and may have cost her the election of 2016. The right is not innocent in the name calling game but when both sides engage in verbal attacks against the collective, it proves to be very divisive. It pits Americans in an "us" verses "them" configuration. It is a reason why many Americans feel that the country has never felt so divided. In fact, a rift not experienced since the Civil War, but it goes beyond that.

It sets up one side as intellectual supremacists and moral judgementalists. Democrats have dominated many of our institutions, from government to the entertainment industry, to the media, to education (the one area I believe conservatives regret surrendering so easily) and to society. I have been an American citizen for over thirty years, but as a conservative I have never felt so much a foreigner as in my own country, in recent times.

In 2016, sixty-two million, nine hundred and eighty-four thousand, eight hundred and twenty-eight Americans voted Donald Trump into office as the President of the United States. Twenty minutes after his inauguration the Washington Post wrote an article calling for his impeachment. In 2008, many people in this country disagreed with the election and the governance of Barack Obama but as he himself stated, "Elections have consequences so get over it."

And he was right, and we conservatives tried to do just *that*, as we gritted our teeth, every time he lectured us and then accomplished very little. Conservatives won some seats back in the mid-term election and used this to check Obama's powers whenever they could, under the constitutional framework. In some instances, these procedures were successful in blocking Obama from advancing his agenda. But they did it under the rules that the framers had designed, and for the most part conservatives respected the office of the President. However, when they did criticize the policies of Obama's administration they had to endure being labeled "racist."

I experienced this personally. I was a white teacher that went to teach in a low-income, Title I school that was 99% black and Hispanic. I was the only white guy for miles around. I do not know of too many racists who would have agreed to put themselves in that kind of position. When Obama got elected there was jubilation throughout the school, as was to be expected. For the first time in history, an African-American had captured the highest office in the country. I was proud that I lived in a country where such a thing could actually happen.

Naturally as a conservative, I was disappointed that our candidate had not prevailed, however I accepted the results and was willing to give the new president an open mind, even though I had real concerns about his inexperience. The school held a rally in our auditorium to celebrate the election and praise the new incoming president. I attended that rally, and despite the fact, that I was polite and respectful, I was accused of being a racist; apparently because I wasn't doing hand stands and back flips in the aisle.

And, in spite of this, there was no hatred on the part of conservatives; there was no resistance movement; there was no Obama derangement syndrome and there was no constant impeachment obsession. Conservatives swallowed their disappointment and rode out the eight years of Obama, as best they could. We waited until we prevailed under the democratic constitutional process and duly elected the next president. Sixty-three million Americans exercised their constitutional right—a right on which this republic was founded-- to conduct a free and fair election.

Donald Trump was elected president and "elections have consequences, so get over it." But unfortunately, the left cannot. But this has evolved into more than calling Trump and his supporters names, it has evolved into more than the resistance or the Trump derangement syndrome, it has evolved into more than impeachment.

The evolution ends and the revolution begins with any illegitimate removal of Donald Trump from office. For conservatives, Donald Trump is the lynchpin, the firewall. He has shown conservatives how to push back. He is the only thing standing between our conservative values and being swamped by a tidal wave of socialist policies proposed by Democrats. Policies that will sweep away the freedoms that we have lived under since the very inception of this country. The conservative views this as a death knell for the future of our democracy. There are two bastions left in this country, that I believe the right will defend to the last breath, and they are the right to bear arms and the right to vote freely in a fair election.

Anything that undermines the election process will be construed as a loss of freedom. Any attempt to sabotage Donald Trump, will be seen as a loss of freedom. And any attempt to remove Trump from office in any way, before this election, will be seen as a nullification of sixty-three million Americans and a loss of freedom. And that *will* cause a firestorm. It has been shown that if there is any one thing that Americans will commit to, it is fighting and dying for their freedom. I say with the certainty of the precedents outlined in this book, that this country will engage in another civil war to preserve freedom.

That is the crux of this book.

Professor Lawrence Tribe on the Chris Matthews show on November 14, 2019 said this "anybody who votes for Trump is a disgusting human being."

Professor Lawrence Tribe has characterized me as a "disgusting human being" because I voted for Donald Trump. I wasn't alone--I had sixty-three million cohorts so by a logical extension sixty-three million "disgusting" fellow "human beings".

But we all know that Professor Tribe is not condemning me for my vote. He is really condemning me for the "smelly Walmart" shopper that I am. He is condemning me for the "Ghost in the sky" and Noah and the Ark "fairytale" believer that I am. Both sides want to condemn the other side for who they are. That is the *real* danger our country faces. That is why according to Joe Biden the very next election will be for the soul of this country. Biden is not right very often, but in this he has never been *so* right.

I just have this to offer to Mr. Tribe and others who want to emulate this tactic.

I was raised by hardworking parents who worked all their lives, earned everything they had and were never given anything in life. Never once did they ever rely on government assistance. My father risked his life for his country and to protect its freedoms as a tail gunner in a B52, in the war against Germany. My mother worked as a nurse in critical care units and took us kids to church every Sunday. I was raised to honor the same work ethic and to follow the precept to be guided by doing the right thing. For 15 years I have served the youth of this country as a special education teacher and mental health counsellor, teaching the kind of students few other teachers wanted to teach, in situations that few other teachers wanted to go and often for very little pay. I was guided by the ideal of trying to make their lives a little better, if I could. Because I exercised my constitutional right to vote for someone, who some ivory tower Harvard professor disapproves, my heritage is desecrated, and my entire life of accomplishments is condensed into a simple three word condemnation "disgusting human being." This is the kind of man to whom we are entrusting the education of our children.

And we wonder why this country is so divided.

And *this* is what happens when one has to hide their conservative viewpoint in the shadows for most of their working life. This is what a conservative looks like when they finally decide enough is enough. This is what a conservative viewpoint sounds like when it is finally set free. This was the emcee of the Golden Globe Awards addressing the Hollywood elitists.

> "It's the last time, who cares? Apple roared into the TV game with The Morning Show, a superb drama about the importance of dignity and doing the right thing, made by a company that runs sweatshops in China. Well, you say you're woke but the companies you work for in China—unbelievable. Apple, Amazon, Disney. If ISIS started a streaming service, you'd call your agent, wouldn't you?
>
> So if you do win an award tonight, don't use it as a platform to make a political speech. You're in no position to lecture the public about anything. You know nothing about the real world. Most of you spent less time in school than Greta Thunberg.
>
> So if you win, come up, accept your little award, thank your agent, and your God and **** off, Ok?"
> Ricky Gervais Golden Globe Awards monologue 1/5/2020

And we wonder why the country is so divided.

Preamble to the U.S. Declaration of Independence, **1776**.

We hold these truths to be self-evident, that all men are created equal, that they are endowed, by their Creator, with certain unalienable Rights, that among these are Life, Liberty, and the pursuit of Happiness

THE AMERICAN REVOLUTION

"This country with its institutions, belongs to the people who inhabit it. Whenever they shall grow weary of the existing government, they can exercise their Constitutional right of amending it, or their revolutionary right to dismember it or over- throw it." Abraham Lincoln

"Give me liberty or give me death." Patrick Henry

Why are we beginning with the American Revolution, you might ask? This was not a civil war, but in effect it was. Why include the Revolutionary War in this context? Civil wars, revolutions and rebellions are not always easy to distinguish from each other, and it can often depend on who the victor is, that determines what label is applied. For instance, in the war between the North and South, the Southerners were considered rebels and traitors because they lost. In the War for Independence the colonists who opposed British rule were called rebels and traitors as well, but since they won, they evolved into patriots.

So, the lines and terms describing these conflicts are often blurred, but I contend that the war for our independence was a revolution in name only. It was essentially an internal civil war between Loyalists and rebels--the only difference from the Civil War being, that in the end, we gained our independence from a particular form of government. In fact, in its first year, it was referred to as a civil war. However, the definitions and terminology are relatively unimportant. What is significant is that in each of the three conflicts that are germane to the premise of this book--there is a pattern of protocol that is always the same. And the American Revolution by following that protocol established the template that the other conflicts emulated.

This is a formula that has been tried and tested over hundreds of years and the first element is freedom. Freedom is at the core, whether it is a case of having no freedom and trying to achieve it, or having a taste of freedom and trying to acquire more, or having a full dose of freedom and trying to preserve it, in the face of a threat that it might be taken away. It is always about freedom.

America was founded on the spirit of freedom, as we saw with the Pilgrims and early pioneers who came to this country, who just wanted to be free to live their lives and practice their religion as they saw fit. I would go so far as to say, that England was destined to lose their colonies the minute that the first English settler landed in America.

That's the funny thing about freedom. Once you get a taste of it, there's no going back. The colonists got used to being independent and living in relative freedom and they only wanted more of it. They recoiled at the idea of being dictated to by a central authority that was 3000 miles of ocean away. They were done with that.

Some historians have even gone so far as to opine that Britain had every right to ask for reparations for their participation in the French and Indian Wars. After all, they had spent their blood and treasure protecting the American colonies, but the colonists did not like the manner, in which taxes were imposed. They saw it as taxation without representation tyranny, and that was an infringement on their freedom and so some engaged in resistance.

The period of resistance began with the Proclamation of 1763 and included the Sugar Act, the Stamp Act, the Townshend Act, the Quartering Act, the Tea Act and the Intolerable Act which escalated to the Boston tea party, the Boston Massacre, the

1st Continental Congress and the opening of armed hostilities at Lexington and Concord. The resistance/negotiation phase can take on different forms. Sometimes it is appeasement and sometimes it is antagonization. I would characterize the American Revolution version of this phase of the conflict, as a series of actions and reactions.

It was the establishment of a pattern that appears in each of the scenarios in this book. That pattern is defined by the acquisition of freedom, the threat of loss of freedom, a period of resistance/ negotiation and the final phase which entails military conflict. Let's take a brief look at some of the incidents that occurred in America's early years to examine their impact on the process.

The French and Indian War 1756-1763

France had expanded into the Ohio territories and were encroaching on claims and interests of the English Colonies and so the British went to war with both France and Spain. As a result of winning the war, the British acquired France's territories in Canada to the north and Spain's territories in Florida to the south. It essentially removed the European rivals who were in conflict with the English Colonies and opened up the Mississippi territory for future expansion. In the process of financing the military for this conflict, Britain doubled its debt.

The Proclamation of 1763

At the conclusion of the French and Indian War, the British Empire was of a mind to start exercising some controls over their rather autonomous colonies. They proclaimed a line of demarcation utilizing the Appalachian Mountains as a boundary prohibiting settlement to the west. It was a measure designed to regulate westward expansion and caused resentment among the colonists, who for the most part ignored it. It particularly angered George Washington.

Sugar Act 1764

The Sugar Act was the first attempt by the British government to get the colonies to pay a share of the cost to defend them in The French and Indian War, by levying duties on sugar and molasses. It wasn't necessarily the sugar and molasses that was being targeted but these were the ingredients used to make rum. The British government was attempting to raise 100,000 pounds which was one fifth of the cost of the war. Historians contend that it was a justifiable action, in light of the fact, that the colonies benefited the most from the military altercation.

It was significant, for a number of reasons. It signaled the end of colonial tax exempt status but because it was voted into law by the British parliament and the colonies had no representatives in that governing body--they felt they had no say in the matter and this became their familiar refrain throughout all of these taxing measures--no taxation without representation.

One of the secondary goals of this tax was to enable the British to finance a standing army in the colonies, mostly for the future protection of the colonists--but the colonists saw this as an infringement on their freedom. The colonies were beginning to sense that perhaps Britain had allowed them too much freedom in the past, and now they were trying to rein in some of that carte blanche. However, it was a little too late for bronc-busting, because this horse was already out of the barn. A second element of this tax allowed customs officials increased authority, to crack down on black market smuggling by seizing the goods of private citizens. Any citizens accused of this kind of trade could be convicted without a trial by jury. This was a blatant denial of the rights and freedoms of the colonists and they were having none of it. The resistance was on. They boycotted British goods. They avoided paying the tax whenever possible and flooded England with letters of protest. The tax was repealed.

But the game was on.

Stamp Act 1765

The Stamp Act was a tax on printed matter such as legal documents, newspapers and other publications and even playing cards. The colonists responded by boycotting some of these items and mistreating the tax collectors. 'Tar and feathering' was a common practice of this time. This act was repealed.

Quartering Act 1765

Required the colonists to subsidize and house a British standing army in the colonies. The colonists saw this as a serious threat to their freedom and independence. It was regarded as nothing less than martial law.

Townshend Acts 1767

This was designed to tax imports of glass, lead, paper, paint, and tea. These items were chosen because it was felt that it would be difficult for the colonists to manufacture them. Some of the money raised was to pay officials in the colonies to remain loyal to Britain and collect these taxes. Once again, the colonists found ways to do without these items and as tension between Britain and the colonies heightened, Britain sent 2000 troops to the colonies to maintain law and order. The act itself was eventually repealed.

Boston Massacre 1770

The presence of 2000 British troops in a city of only 16,000 colonists was a pressure cooker just waiting to explode. On March 5, 1770, a British soldier was guarding the customs house in Boston when he was heckled by a group of colonists. Other British soldiers came to his aid and the colonists responded by hurling snowballs and rocks at the soldiers. In the ensuing melee, the British soldiers fired into the crowd killing five colonists and wounding six others. The soldiers were arrested, jailed and put on trial. They were acquitted on the grounds that their actions were provoked. The British commander in charge of the troops that day, described it best, "None of them was a hero. The victims were troublemakers who got more than they deserved. The soldiers were professionals...who shouldn't have panicked. The whole thing shouldn't have happened."

Nevertheless, the fallout from this event only served to further incite the rage of the colonists.

Events were spinning out of control.

Tea Act and Boston Tea Party 1773

In an effort, to reduce tensions in Boston, the British moved their troops outside the city and repealed the Townshend Acts. However, a new tax on tea was imposed in 1773. Again, the colonists responded by boycotting English products. When three ships loaded with tea from the British East India Company, arrived in Boston harbor, they were raided in the night by colonists known as the Sons of Liberty, dressed up as Indians. As an act of protest, they tossed 342 chests of tea into the water, costing almost a million dollars of destruction in today's values.

Intolerable Acts 1774

England was not about to let the Boston Tea Party go unpunished. Their retribution was the Intolerable Acts which closed Boston Harbor until restitution for the tea that was destroyed was paid, ended free elections of town officials, established martial law in Massachusetts, and allowed British troops to requisition the homes of private citizens for their own use.

First Continental Congress 1774

Needless to say, the colonists were outraged by the Intolerable Acts, as they viewed them justifiably by their name: intolerable. Thus, they convened delegates from the other colonies in Philadelphia, to act in accordance to the British oppression. They resolved to censure Britain for the Intolerable Acts and demanded their repeal, called for an organized boycott of British goods, proclaimed the right of the colonies to their independence and established the formation of a colonial militia.

Lexington and Concord 1775

On April 18th, 700 British soldiers marched out of Boston with the goal of seizing a cache of munitions and arms that was supposedly hidden in Concord Massachusetts. Being warned that night by Paul Revere and others, the British were intercepted by about 70 colonials on Lexington green. A shot was fired, no one knows from which side it came, and a skirmish ensued. Eight colonials were killed, and the fuse for what would become the American Revolution was lit. This was exemplified by more intense fighting in Concord.

The preceding was a quick summary of events leading to our conflict for independence and was not intended to be a history lesson although if any of this was new then it did serve to educate, which to a former teacher is never a bad thing. But what it does illustrate is that conflict usually does not arise out of a vacuum. It is a process of give and take, sometimes of cause and effect, sometimes of retribution and appeasement, that escalates to a flashpoint and becomes a full- fledged explosion. This will not be the last time you see this pattern develop when people are on the march to civil unrest.

Definition of lynchpin: A central and cohesive source of stability and security; a person or thing that is critical to a system or organization.

The other takeaway from this conflict was the emergence of George Washington as the original American lynchpin even before America was officially recognized as a country. Washington was on board with the revolution from the beginning. He supported the separation and conflict early on when many of his countrymen had not yet joined the cause. Washington had garnered much land from his service in the French and Indian wars and the Proclamation of 1763 restricted his use of those lands. Much of Washington's wealth was tied up in land and he felt it was unjust what Britain was dictating to the American colonists.

It was Washington who organized and trained an underdog rag tag bunch of militiamen and led them against the most powerful army in the world. It was Washington who crafted the escape of his revolutionary army when they were trapped in New York and saved them from annihilation. Had it not been for Washington's guile the revolution would have been over right then and there. It was Washington who engineered the surprise attack at Trenton that resulted in a victory and changed the course of events for the American cause. And it was Washington who held the army together in the face of starvation and desertion at Valley Forge. In that dire winter where over 1000 soldiers starved to death and the dissolution of the army was imminent, Washington saw them through. Just as a side note, Washington also had to endure threats and secret plots against him from within his own ranks—a common thread that Lincoln and Trump would face in the course of their administrations and another element that binds the three of them under the mantle of lynchpin.

Eventually Washington would lead his army to a miraculous victory over the most powerful army in the world. He became the first president of the new country and established many of the protocols for governance. His seminal achievement might be that he rejected assuming the powers of kingship when they were readily available to him. There would be no America today if not for George Washington, unarguably the first American lynchpin.

Gettysburg Address November 19, 1863.

Four score and seven years ago our fathers brought forth on this continent, a new nation, conceived in liberty, and dedicated to the proposition that all men are created equal. Now we are engaged in a great civil war, testing whether that nation, or any nation so conceived and so dedicated, can long endure. We are met on a great battlefield of that war. We have come to dedicate a portion of that field, as a final resting place for those who gave their lives that the nation might live. It is altogether fitting that we should do this. But in a larger sense, we cannot dedicate, we cannot consecrate, we cannot hallow this ground. The brave men, living and dead, who struggled here, have consecrated it far beyond our poor power to add or detract. The world will little note, nor long remember, what we say here, but it can never forget what they did here. It is for us the living, rather, to be dedicated here to the unfinished work which they who have fought here have thus far so nobly advanced. It is rather for us to be here dedicated to the great task remaining before us. That from these honored dead we raise increased devotion, that cause for which they gave the last full measure of devotion – that here we highly resolve that these dead shall not have died in vain--that this nation, under God, shall have a new birth of freedom--and that government of the people, by the people, for the people, shall not perish from the earth.

Abraham Lincoln

1ˢᵗ AMERICAN CIVIL WAR

"We are engaged in a great civil war." These were the words of Abraham Lincoln on November 19, 1863 at the dedication of a cemetery at Gettysburg, Pennsylvania to bury some of the 53,000 casualties that had occurred during three days of fighting between the North and the South.

These are probably the most horrific words that a president of a country would ever have to utter and the most chilling for its citizens, to ever have to bear.

The Civil War was unquestionably the most divisive event in our country's history. When the citizens of a country have resorted to killing each other en masse as the last measure to solving their differences, that I would say by any measure, is inherently divisive. You would *think* that would have set an indelible precedent, never to be repeated. You would *think* that history would have taught us to avoid the same mistakes that once took this country down the path to civil war but, unfortunately, I am afraid that the current situation in America, in many ways, parallels elements of the Civil War. Almost to the point of guaranteeing, that a second altercation will be inevitable, if we continue down our present course. I am convinced to a certainty that Lincoln's words will resonate once more across this land.

When you think about that time in our history, it is truly amazing, that we could have reached such a lethal level of animosity toward each other. This was a special brand of hatred not seen before, that cut across all segments of society on the American landscape (although I imagine what our European ancestors did to the American Indians evoked a similar kind of raw emotion).

This was a hatred that did not just divide North and South but reached deep into families. It pitted rich against poor, friend against friend and brother against brother and it is still evident to this day in some instances. The question is, have we reached that same level of hatred today?

Ironically, for the North, this was not a war to free the slaves, at least not initially, but it was a war about freedom. It was always about that for the South and nothing else. The war was the manifestation to take away the freedom to conduct their way of life. Since the majority of it, was fought in southern territory, it physically destroyed their homeland. Sherman's March to the sea and scorched earth policy which extended the conflict to civilians and was designed to make the South "howl", also exacerbated the hatred of Southerners. After the war, northern carpet baggers swooped in and unfairly took advantage of a devasted and vulnerable Southland. All of these things fueled a deep and profound hatred of the South for their Northern countrymen.

Even today in the South the term "yankee" which refers to a Northerner, takes on a negative connotation. And many Southerners still refer to the Civil War as "the war of Northern aggression." But it was much worse than name calling and turning phrases. The citizens of this country took up arms against each other with the sole purpose of collectively annihilating the other side. Why? Because we could not come to a suitable agreement? Was there no compromise that could have defused it? How could this happen?

People have disagreements all the time and most of the time they don't end up killing each other over their differences. Although many times they do, as evidenced by the prevalence of war, since the beginning of humanity. People will always find differences with each other. I saw this firsthand when I taught school.

My first job as a teacher was in a Title I public school in the Bronx, New York where the population of the school was 98% African American and Hispanic. I had spent the majority of my adult life, up to that point in the very homogenously white state of New Hampshire. I had very little experience interacting with minorities, so I guess in that sense, I was fairly naive. I was certainly unsophisticated when it came to discerning the different shadings of skin pigment. To my unpracticed eye, I only saw white or dark skin.

I was about to be taken to task. One day, during a lesson I was calling on the students in my class to answer questions I was posing to them. Students would raise their hand if they thought they had the correct answer and I would select one of them. We continued in this manner for a period of time, until at one point, a student asked a question of me.

"Mr. Sneider" he said, "Are you a racist?"

I have to say I was quite taken aback by the question. In my mind I couldn't think of one thing that I had done to warrant such an accusation.

"Why would you ask such a question?" I responded.

"Because you are only picking "them" to answer the questions."

"What do you mean by that? Who is "them"?"

Then, this African-American student said "Why are you only picking the Latinos every time and never one of us?"

I was floored. I was just picking students randomly or at least I thought I was. It had never occurred to me that within the context of these "dark" skinned students there were varying degrees of "darkness" which I was, at least at that point, unable to distinguish.

I was blown away. Racism as I had understood it, had always been about discrimination between white and black people and there were no white students in my class so how could I be racist. Now I had a new definition. It was a somber lesson that I had learned the hard way. It was my theory that even when you think people are similar in most ways, they have a tendency to focus on what makes them different.

I realized that the reason one group will emphasize a difference, no matter how small is to use that difference to make themselves appear superior.

I saw this theory play out in the halls of this school almost every day. There were no uniforms in this school and it was a very poor neighborhood. And yet a lot of these students somehow were able to afford expensive, brand name sneakers. It was the ultimate status symbol. I can't tell you the number of times I witnessed a student being teased (unmercifully at times) because they didn't have the "right" kind of sneakers. I can understand why some schools adopt a dress uniform to eliminate this kind of discrimination.

And unfortunately, people will use differences as one of many excuses to kill.

But a civil war is a special kind of entity. The combatants are all members of a similar set of society. In the case of America, we were all united in a common cause to revolt against Great Britain and form our own country – although truth be told, it was only one-third of the country in favor of independence at the beginning of the revolution. But by its end we were united in a common cause for which we fought and died. And that bonded us in a way that just living in a common geographic area never could.

We had fought and died to secure our independence from what we perceived was a tyrannical system of government. We had prevailed against overwhelming odds and now we were free to pursue our own conception of how people should be governed. We did that with our Constitution. No more kings and no more caste systems.

Every individual was free to pursue life, liberty and happiness. And that "of the people, by the people and for the people" was the great experiment that once again bonded us in a way that was unique to other countries. Noble thoughts and words indeed.

We wrote some of these very words in the documents that became the framework for how this country was to be incorporated.

So again, I posed the question, how did we become so divided against our beloved countrymen that we sought their demise? The answer is that the subject of our disagreement must have been of a uniquely special nature. It must have been irreconcilable. And as it turned out, indeed it was. It was the issue of slavery. It was the exception that the framers overlooked when they drafted the Constitution.

A couple of myths need to be dispelled at this point. The controversy over slavery did not happen overnight. It was an evolutionary process that had all the colonies with 'skin in the game' to make a bad pun, in terms of total acquiescence and participation when slavery was conceived in America. And secondly, we never fought the Civil War over the abolition of slavery or State's rights, for that matter, but I submit it was fought over freedom.

Yes, there is no denying that the Civil War was fought over the issue of slavery but for the North it was not to free them. Lincoln never proposed that slavery be abolished prior to becoming president but he did want to restrict its expansion and he ran for election with that as his platform.

For Lincoln it was all about preserving the union.

> "If I could save the Union without freeing any slave I would do it, and if I could save it by freeing all the slaves I would do it: and if I could save it by freeing some and leaving others alone I would also do that."

("and that government of the people, by the people, for the people, shall not perish from the earth.")

And he was willing to go to war to preserve that union. Later, it would also encompass freedom for slaves, in the form of The Emancipation Proclamation. For the South, although slavery was an underlying cause, it was about their freedom to live their lives as they saw fit AND to own slaves.

SLAVERY

Northern Viewpoint attributed to Joshua Chamberlain Union army officer.

"This is a different kind of army. If you look at history, you'll see men fight for pay, or women or some other kind of loot. They fight for land, or because a king makes them, or just because they like killing. But we're here for something new. I don't ... this hasn't happened much in the history of the world. We're an army going out to set other men free."

"This is free ground. All the way from here to the Pacific Ocean. No man has to bow. No man born to royalty. Here we judge you by what you do, not by what your father was. Here you can be something. Here's a place to build a home. It isn't the land-there's always more land. It's the idea that we all have value, you and me, we're worth something more than the dirt. I never saw dirt I'd die for, ...what we're all fighting for, in the end, is each other."

Southern viewpoint attributed to George Pickett, Confederate army officer.

"...what a shame it was that so many people seemed to think it was slavery that brought on the war, when all it was really was a question of the Constitution. ...Actually, I think my analogy of the club was the best. I mean, it's as if we all joined a gentleman's club, and then the members of the club started sticking their noses into our private lives, and then we up and resigned, and then they tell us we don't have the right to resign.... You must tell them, and make it plain, that what we are fighting for is our freedom from the rule of what is to us a foreign government. That's all we want and that's what this war is *all* about. We established this country in the first place with strong state governments just for that reason, to avoid a central tyranny... know that government derives its power from the consent of the governed. Every government, everywhere. And sir, let me make this plain: We do not consent. We will never consent."

The analogy from the Southern viewpoint was surely applicable in its own sense but I would be more inclined to liken the situation to a marital arrangement. Hypothetically, it starts with two single people who enjoy the independence and freedoms that the single life affords. But then, they decide to join forces and enter into a union, for what may be a number of possible reasons. Perhaps they want to pool their financial resources or perhaps they want a platform to start a family. There are certain benefits that a marital union offers, that a single life can't provide, but with those benefits comes increased responsibilities-some legal and some implied.

As the union progresses, it is only natural that there will be differences of opinion. It is inherent in the human condition, that no two people will always be in agreement, on everything. How these disagreements are handled becomes the crux of the matter. Some may be resolved and some may not. Perhaps the ones that are not, are left to fester. Maybe they cause resentment and maybe this results in changes of behavior that are detrimental to the health of the relationship.

Perhaps, such issues as trust, understanding and certain rules agreed upon at the beginning of the union, are infringed upon or violated. At this point, the couple may seek intervention from outside sources, in the form of advice from family and friends, or perhaps a more independent arbiter such as a marriage counsellor. In some cases, some of these measures might work and the situation might defuse, but in other cases it might only serve as temporary stopgaps or prove to totally ineffective altogether. Perhaps at this point the discord escalates.

None of the mitigating factors have succeeded and one or both of the parties might deem the situation irreconcilable. To remain together any longer, would only invite more discord and perhaps even escalation of a physical nature. At this point, physical separation is the preferable course of action and the courts allow for just such a legal recourse.

It's called a divorce.

I wish I could say that this was the end of the matter and in most cases a divorce is the end of the acrimony, but in some cases, it is not an end, and domestic violence can occur beyond the end of the union. Especially if one of the parties cannot accept the decision of the court, or the terms of the divorce.

I know this is a simplistic characterization of a marital relationship, but it does have parallels and applications to a dispute on a larger scale. We saw this in our revolution, and we will see it again.

Initially, slavery was not a controversial issue in the founding of this country. Slavery existed all over the world, before a European ever set foot on American soil. Conquering nations routinely enslaved the population of vanquished nations, as far back as the written word and Biblical times. Who do you think built the Egyptian pyramids? The Roman empire was built on the backs of slaves. In the Americas, Inca and Aztec sacrificial instruments were drenched with the blood of slaves.

No one was better at enslavement than Nazi Germany. They were one of the best at overpowering a country through military force and then enslaving their vanquished enemies. They would employ that slave labor to do the manual tasks, that would free the men of Germany to do the fighting, although the slaves could be impressed to do that as well. Most of the Atlantic Wall, which was designed to repel the D-day invasion was built with slave labor.

It is the very nature of nature that conflict produces a victor and a loser, and the loser is submissive to the will of the victor. It is a natural law in the animal world. This is codified as the survival of the fittest. In translation a victor becomes a predator and the loser becomes the prey. Conflict is the natural byproduct of human interaction. Human beings are not insulated from this basic law of nature either, although in most cases the conquerors do not eat their fellow vanquished. Cannibals would be the exception. It is only in rare instances that a conquering nation, if they do not kill the vanquished do *not* impose their will on them in some form, of which slavery would be the most restrictive.

This also explains why freedom is such a rare and valuable commodity, in any of the societal structures of the world. How many countries even today have citizens who consider themselves to be free? But I digress, the point is that slavery/caste system and other societal structures are present even within citizens of their own countries and so it is no surprise, that strength and might cause weaker opponents to be forced into submission.

In a world of extreme manual labor, free or cheap workers are in high demand. It was the way that powerful nations in the past built, expanded and stayed powerful. America in its infancy, was no different. It was a very different time in which the institution of slavery was accepted, and everyone was complicit.

Slaves or indentured servants came over on the first boats to land on the shores of America; those of Columbus and the Mayflower. Cortez and the Spanish explorers made slaves of the Native Americans. Slaves were imported from Africa to work in America's tobacco farms of Virginia, cotton farms of the Carolinas, ports of the North and sugarcane fields of the West Indies. It is one of the greatest myths of all, that the majority of the slave trade that came out of Africa went to America. In truth only a small percentage went to the American colonies. 12.5 million slaves were extracted from Africa. Almost 2 million died during the Middle Passage. Of the 10.5 million that survived only 388,000 (about 3.6%) arrived in North America with the rest going to the West Indies and South America.

It should be noted that slavery was embroidered in the fabric of America, from its first threads, and was just as prevalent and accepted in the North as it was in the South. The Declaration of Independence, the Constitution and the Bill of Rights did nothing to change this. Even though the phrase "all men are created equal" was a cornerstone of these documents, many of the authors and framers and even presidents, did not adhere to these principles.

The reason for this obvious and blatant contradiction was that the slaves were not considered to be "men" but inferior and relegated to "property," "contraband," and "chattel." However, in a cruel twist of fate, for the apportionment of representation purposes only, slaves were counted as 3/5 of a person thus enabling some white politician from the South to vote on behalf of enslaved people for the perpetuation of slavery.

It was the industrialization of the North, that rendered its dependence of slave labor less addictive. Factory owners in the North, actually preferred to use the influx of immigrants coming from Europe at this time because they did not have to provide for their care, and they could tailor their workforce to efficiently get through booms and busts.

At the same time, the invention of the cotton gin caused an explosion of the slave trade in the South because now that more cotton could be ginned faster, it meant more cotton could be planted and cultivated and that required more manual labor.

Then of course there was the book "Uncle Tom's Cabin" and the abolition movement was born. It did seem to be somewhat convenient that now that the reliance on slave labor had diminished in the North, due mostly to the external factors, that now it became undesirable to participate in slavery on purely moral grounds. It is a lot easier to give up something when you do not really need it anymore. Unfortunately for the South, slavery was baked into their economy and way of life and that is key-- slavery was an integral part of the Southern agrarian lifestyle.

ESCALATION TO CIVIL WAR

Quote by John Brown; "I am now quite certain that the crimes of this guilty land will never be argued away but with blood."

A serial killer, typically, does not start killing others as a first step. There is usually a period of evolution--maybe they start out with small animals then become more violent on an escalating spectrum before graduating to murder. The Civil War was similar in that respect. There were many instances of compromise and attempts to mediate the issues of slavery, over a protracted period of time. Obviously, none of the measures worked and the situation escalated until it became irreconcilable. It was at that point that some would say that the explosion into Civil War was inevitable and all the situation required was a trigger.

That is kind of what happened.

So once again the ideological fray is joined and the pattern of appeasement develops.

1820 Missouri Compromise

Following the 1803 Louisiana Purchase, which almost doubled the size of the country, the population of America began expanding west. Congress was forced to establish a policy to govern the expansion of slavery into the new western territory. A measure was introduced in Congress that would prohibit slavery in the Missouri territory even though it had applied for statehood as a slave state.

Southerners saw this as a measure to limit the expansion of their economy. They needed new land to grow cotton and cotton required slaves. A restriction on slavery was a restriction on their right to prosperity. Forasmuch as it was a moral issue posed by the growth of slavery, the addition of a pro-slavery state would give the pro-slavery faction a majority in Congress. At the time, there were 22 states in the union, equally divided between free and slave. It was the catalyst that sparked an acrimonious national debate. Arthur Livermore of New Hampshire expressed the Northern opinion,

"How long will the desire for wealth render us blind to the sin of holding both the bodies and souls of our fellow men in chains?"

The Western Monitor voiced the Southern view,

"The slaveholding states will not brook an invasion of their rights."

In order to preserve the Congressional balance, a series of agreements were struck that became known as the Missouri Compromise. Missouri was admitted as a slave state and Maine was admitted as a free state. In addition, a demarcation line was drawn through the western territories along the 36°30' parallel. Any new territories that were admitted to the union above that latitude would be free and any that were admitted below the line would be slave.

Thomas Jefferson, "considered it at once as the knell of the Union. But this is a reprieve only, not a final sentence. A geographical line, coinciding with a marked principle, moral and political, once conceived and held up to the angry passions of men, will never be obliterated; and every new irritation will mark it deeper and deeper."

This legislation set the stage for sectionalism over nationalism as both sides feared that each was conspiring to undermine the interests of the other. In its place, states' rights were once again taking increased precedence.

1831 Nat Turner's Rebellion

It was said that Nat Turner was inspired by God and two solar eclipses to rise up.

In 1831, Nat Turner instigated an uprising that encompassed several plantations in Virginia. Turner and seventy fellow slaves killed around fifty-five white people. The bloody rampage was finally quelled by militia after two days of terror.

Turner and sixteen of his cohorts, were tried and hung for their role in the insurrection. Nearly two hundred more were lynched in the aftermath. Although previously there had been small-scale slave uprisings in the South this was the most notable and in the face of increasing abolitionist rhetoric from the North, it led to new laws restricting freedom of speech and the press. It also led to severe restrictions on the education of slaves and the right to assemble.

1846-1850 The Wilmot Proviso

Tensions between pro-slavery and anti-slavery factions increased during a war with Mexico. Under the cloak of Manifest Destiny—a belief that America was entitled to inherit the continent from sea to sea—by conquest if necessary. The conflict with Mexico presented just such an opportunity for the acquisition of new land if the Americans could prevail. As both the South and the North eyed this new territory the question of whether slavery would be permitted once again reared its ugly head.

The Wilmot Proviso was legislation proposed by David Wilmot at the end of the Mexican-American War. The Proviso would have outlawed slavery in territory acquired by the United States as a result of the war. Despite two years of trying to get the bill passed, it never became law. However, the volatility of the debate centering around the Proviso prompted the first intimations of secession. When the bill was brought to a vote it was not voted on party lines but as Northerners and Southerners. A northern newspaper wrote of the proviso, "As if by magic, it brought to a head the great question which is about to divide the American people."

1850 The Compromise of 1850

The Wilmot Proviso had left a bad taste in the mouth of the country, but it was about to get worse. After the Mexican War, Mexico ceded nearly 1 million square miles of territory and so the question of what to do with it, in regard to slavery, was once again posed. The rhetoric heated up. John Hale of New Hampshire said, "If this Union with all its advantages, has no other cement than the blood of human slavery, let it perish!"

Alexander Stephens of Georgia responded, "Principles, sir, are not only outposts, but the bulwarks of all Constitutional liberty; and if these are yielded or taken by superior force, the citadel will soon follow."

If the language was any indication of the sentiment, the country appeared to be on the brink of dissolution.

Senators Henry Clay and Stephen Douglas managed to cobble a shaky appeasement with the Compromise of 1850. The compromise allowed California into the union as a free state and agreed that there would be no Congressional intercession in the matter of slavery in the remainder of the Mexican acquired territory all while strengthening the Fugitive Slave Act--a law which compelled Northerners to capture and return escaped slaves to the South.

While the compromise succeeded in postponing open hostilities between the North and South, it did little to defuse, and in some ways even advanced, the structural disparity that divided the United States. The new Fugitive Slave Act, forced non-slaveholders to interact with escaped slaves, further increasing polarization.

Clay issued a final warning on the issue, that secession would mean war, and "to pause at the edge of the precipice, before the fearful and disastrous leap is taken into the yawning abyss below."

1852 Uncle Tom's Cabin

The Fugitive Slave Law had many cities in the North in a state of insurrection and civil disobedience over the practice of slave-catching. Northern officials thwarted the Southern slave-hunters at every turn. The plight of the runaways, as wrenching as it was in real life, was brought to the fore by a fictional account of the suffering of slaves. It was the greatest piece of abolitionist propaganda to date. It brought home the evils of slavery to the average Northerner selling 300,000 copies and Harriett Beecher Stowe's novel became the second best-selling book in America in the 19th century, second only to the Bible. But it only served to enrage Southerners with its stereo-typed characterizations further driving a wedge between the two sections of the country.

1854-1859 Bleeding Kansas

The Kansas-Nebraska Act of 1854 established Kansas and Nebraska as territories and set the table for "Bleeding Kansas". It was the window into the future of the country. The Kansas-Nebraska Act over-rode the tenets of The Missouri Compromise and the 36/30 line by adopting popular sovereignty, even though Kansas was above the line which meant it should be designated as a free state. Under the popular sovereignty concept, it is the residents of the territories who decide by their vote if the state is to be a free or slave. This set up a situation where settlers on both sides of the issue rushed into Kansas to try to impact the decision. Given the passion surrounding the question of slavery, confrontation was inevitable and violence raged.

In 1855, abolitionist John Brown came to Kansas to combat the forces of slavery. Brown and his followers killed five pro-slavery settlers in the Pottawatomie Creek Massacre which ignited a guerilla war between pro-slavery and anti-slavery forces. The violence was punctuated by an incident on the floor of the US Senate, when after delivering an anti -slavery speech he called "The Crime Against

Kansas", Massachusetts Senator, Charles Sumner, was assaulted by Preston Brooks of South Carolina and severely beaten with his cane. It would be more than two years before Sumner would recover from his injuries to return to take his seat in the Senate and until then his empty chair served as a reminder of southern irrationality and violence over the question of slavery. The violence abated in 1859, the warring factions forged a temporary peace, but not before more than 50 settlers had been killed.

1857 Dred Scott

It didn't take long before passions were once again incited. Dred Scott was a Virginia slave who tried to sue for his freedom in court. His owner had taken him to live in free states and Scott maintained that he was now free on that basis.

Chief Justice Roger Taney proclaimed blacks "so far inferior that they had no rights which the white man was bound to respect."

As to his freedom, Taney ruled that as a slave, Dred Scott was a piece of property and slaveholders had a right to take their property into the territories. Scott had lost his suit on all counts. The sectional divisions only intensified. Taney was vilified by the North. The South felt vindicated and issued new challenges to territorial limitations on slavery. The classification of slaves as property cast doubt on the federal government's authority to regulate slavery.

1858 Lincoln-Douglas Debates

In 1858, Democratic Senator Stephen Douglas ran against Abraham Lincoln. Lincoln and Douglas engaged in seven public debates across the state of Illinois where they debated the most controversial issue of the time: slavery. These debates catapulted Lincoln to the national spotlight, exposed some of his positions and gave him a platform for his nomination for president in 1860. However for Douglas, the debates served to alienate him from the southern components of the Democratic Party and his arguments locked him into a platform that made Douglas unelectable in 1860.

1859 John Brown's Raid

Even after John Brown had eventually stood down from the violence in Kansas, his fervor against slavery had only intensified and had not stopped him from plotting more violence. His plan was to take a group of 19 supporters to Harper's Ferry, Virginia and raid the federal arsenal. With the acquired weapons, he would be able to arm slaves and lead them in an insurrection. It was a plan of action that would propel him into the role of a catalyst for war. Brown was able to capture the armory but when no slaves joined his forces, the insurrection was doomed to fail.

A force of U.S. Marines, led by Col. Robert E. Lee, put down the uprising. Both sides suffered casualties; seven people were killed. Brown and seven of his remaining men were captured. On October 27, Brown was tried for treason against the state of Virginia, convicted and hanged. John Brown became a martyr in death.

"Now if it is deemed necessary that I should forfeit my life for the furtherance of the ends of justice, and mingle my blood further with the blood of my children and with the blood of millions in this slave country...I say let it be done."

"To many Southerners, this was an endorsement of the atrocity and meant that they had better prepare to fight." Time Life Books

1860 Abraham Lincoln's Election

Abraham Lincoln was elected president in 1860.

"On the one hand, he said, neither he nor the Republican Party sought to interfere with slavery in those states where it existed. On the other, slavery was, in his view, a dreadful wrong, a denial of the American principle that all men are created equal."

As a Republican, his party's perceived anti-slavery platform struck fear into many Southerners.

Southerners expressed their concern "Rather than submit to such humiliation and degradation as the inauguration of Abraham Lincoln, the South would see the Potomac crimsoned in human gore, and Pennsylvania Avenue paved ten fathoms deep with mangled bodies."

On December 20, 1860, barely a month after the polls closed, South Carolina seceded from the Union. Six more states followed by the spring of 1861.

"We are divorced, North and South, because we have hated each other so." Mary Chestnut

1861 The Battle of Fort Sumter

With the advent of secession, several federal forts, including Fort Sumter in South Carolina, found themselves to be outposts in a foreign land. Abraham Lincoln chose to re-supply his batteries.

On April 12, 1861, Confederate warships repelled the supply convoy to Fort Sumter and open up their guns on the fortress. The garrison surrendered on April 14.

The Civil War was now joined.

"The guns had spoken. Like the sword that cut the Gordian knot, the Confederate cannon had sliced through the tangle of issues that reasonable men had failed to unsnarl for a half century and more. No longer would Northerners and Southerners have to grapple with the agonizing issues of slavery and state's rights, or with the rough-cut attempts to reconcile those issues. To the immense relief of many, the men of the North and the South were finally free to settle their differences in the simplest way—by force of arms." Time Life Books

It is ironic that not only was President Lincoln the trigger for the Civil War, but also the lynchpin that kept the Union together throughout the war. Once it was known that Lincoln would become the next president in 1860, the South starting with South Carolina, began declaring their succession from the Union. It was their belief that the election of Lincoln was the death knell for the institutions of slavery and the way of life in the South, even though Lincoln and the Republicans never claimed that they were out to abolish slavery.

However, they openly admitted that part of their platform was to restrict the spread of slavery into the new territories but leave it alone where it was already established. Why was this stance so threatening to the South? Did it not appear that slavery under the Republican regime was protected for the time being and any changes to it were certainly not imminent? The South saw it differently. To understand this, we must look into the culture of the South. The first reason was rooted in geography.

The climate and the geography of our southern territory always predisposed it to be an agrarian society as opposed to the rockier terrain of the North and its shorter growing season. And those are exactly the economic lines that evolved.

The North became more industrialized taking the place of the English markets for Southern raw materials after the Revolution. The industrial component of this kind of symbiotic relationship always seems to regard itself as superior to the supplier component. The North looked upon themselves as the transformers of raw goods into finished products that were essential to everyone's quality of life.

Just as when we were the Colonies supplying raw materials to the English factories, they were the parent and America was looked upon as the impetuous child. Now the same relationship was applied to the North and South; with the South engaged in a constant fight since the Revolution to get the North to treat it as an equal. This inferiority complex was very real in the eyes of the South. The South saw intellectual supremacists and moral judge-mentalists.

1851 editorial from a Southern newspaper

> "We purchase all our luxuries and necessities from the North. Our slaves are clothed with Northern manufactured goods, have Northern hats and shoes, work with Northern hoes, plows and other implements. The

slaveholder dresses in Northern goods, rides in a Northern saddle, sports his Northern carriage, reads Northern books. In Northern vessels his products are carried to market, his cotton is ginned with Northern gins, his sugar is crushed and preserved with Northern machinery, his rivers are navigated by Northern steamboats. His son is educated at a Northern college his daughter receives the finishing polish at a Northern seminary, his doctor graduates at a Northern medical college, his schools are furnished with Norther teachers, and he is furnished with Northern inventions."

However, even when the South tried to diversify and provide some balance to their economy, they were at the mercy of Northern banks who refused to invest in Southern enterprises because their workforce was based on slave labor.

"In the view of many Southerners, the South had become a hapless colonial region that was exploited by the industrialized North. 'Financially, we are more enslaved than our Negroes,' complained an Alabamian." Time-Life Books

Part of the inequity in the South stemmed from the *way* they managed their geography.

The South practiced single crop farming versus crop rotation, and this took a toll on the productivity of the soil. In order to stay profitable and maintain higher productivity levels, new land was constantly needed for cultivation.

However, if slavery were restricted from expansion into these new lands then the agricultural economy itself of southern farmers would be drastically curtailed. Not to mention their political power. As more free states were admitted to the Union the balance of power in Congress would shift. The concerns of the Southern plantations would diminish along with their political clout and they would always be at the mercy of the Northern states.

As the South saw it, slavery would eventually die out and they were not about to let that happen and they did not want a bunch of high-on-their-horse Northerners, taking away their freedoms and telling them how to live. It is funny how it always comes down to freedom, especially when you are talking about Americans.

The South was feeling the same threat to their freedom and they decided that there was no longer a resolution to the question of slavery, so they seceded. It is ironic that perceiving a threat to their freedom to conduct their way of life was sufficient to cause succession, when that way of life was based on the suppression of freedom of a whole race of people.

It is also important to note that war was not a goal of the South. All the South wanted was to secede and be left alone to conduct their own affairs. There was no expression of aggression and arguably there would have been no civil war if Lincoln had acquiesced to their wishes. At least, not at the time that it occurred. This is a distinction of paramount import and it will come into play again. One question left to ponder about slavery is "if the confederacy had been allowed to secede how would and when would the institution of slavery been abolished assuming that it would not have been allowed to continue to the present?"

But Lincoln was all about saving the Union and succession was not an option. And so, we branded the act of succession, treasonous and our fellow citizens as rebels and traitors and we backed the South into a corner. And even though it was the South that fired the first shot it was the North that advocated for physical aggression as the final solution. On that basis, all-out war became inevitable. And we already know that Americans will readily die for freedom as we saw in the war for our independence– and on the prison ships.

Reconstruction

> "The slave went free, stood for a brief moment in the
> sun, then moved back again into slavery."
> W.E.B. DuBois

When the war ended the South was in physical shambles. The majority of the war had taken place in Confederate territory. The destruction of the South was almost total. I don't believe that the next civil war will be as confined. I don't believe that in the next civil war, we would get off so lightly. In terms of human cost, over one quarter of all southern white men were dead. At the start of the war the Confederacy had 297 towns or cities with a population of 835,000 people not including slaves. By the end of the war, 162 of the towns or cities with 681,000 people had come into contact with union forces. Eleven of these cities effectively suffered complete devastation.

Farms were in bad shape as well. Forty percent of livestock had been killed. Farm equipment had also been devalued by 40 %. The infrastructure of the transportation systems had been almost completely destroyed leaving no practical means to get farm products to market. The costs of this physical damage totaled over $3 billion. The confederate dollar had been rendered worthless by rampant inflation and the banking system was depleted. Needless to say, poverty was pervasive throughout the South and it was in desperate need of reconstruction.

Practically overnight, with the conclusion of the Civil War, almost 4 million slaves gained their freedom. If you think that went well, think again. It was one of the most difficult periods in the history of the country. It was the ultimate reset. The first question was what to do with 4 million former slaves.

Lincoln was never a fervent abolitionist even though he witnessed slavery all around him. His strongest conviction was that every man was entitled to the fruits of his labor, and slavery robbed a man of that right. But Lincoln never set out to free one single slave. As the head of the Republican party, he ran on the platform of not allowing slavery to expand into new territory, but he was always committed to save the Union. His statement, his sentiment was that he would free none of the slaves, he would free all of them or he would free just one of the slaves to keep the Union together. Abolition of slavery evolved later as the war progressed, and lent the cause a nobleness, but even in the wake of abolition some of the options of what was to be done with the slaves once they were free, were not exactly as noble as was the sentiment to free them.

One option was to integrate, but one option called for segregation, and a third option called for deportation to Africa in the state of Liberia. The American Colonization Society was founded some 50 years before the majority of slaves were freed, with the purpose of acquiring land in West Africa for settlement by African-Americans. In its first 40 years 12,000 free black men and former slaves were shipped there and it became the nation of Liberia in 1847. Lincoln favored this third option as late as 1862, as he didn't believe that whites and blacks could co-exist equally in the same country. It was one thing to free the slaves, but in reality, nobody, not even Abraham Lincoln himself, wanted them to be living among them once they were free. Lincoln would later abandon this position, once he realized that all the slaves were going to be free at once, and it would prove to be logistically impossible to transport that many at once.

But the priority for Lincoln was always that he wanted the nation to endure--he stated that in the Gettysburg address and he succeeded in that endeavor. He was the lynchpin that kept the country together, despite the wishes of one side to dissolve the Union and the bloody war that followed, and once he declared a new birth of freedom with the Emancipation Proclamation--it became a war that would free other men. Half the country was willing to fight and die for them and that was unique. And up to that point, what conflict was there that had men fighting and dying to provide freedom for another group of men?

In the end, the victory of the Union army resulted in a country that was truly embracing the principle that all its citizens were free. A freedom that had been proclaimed in theory in the preamble to the Declaration of Independence, but never fulfilled in practice. So, in summary the war for the Union forces was fought for freedom. And in the South the misconception was that the war was fought for the preservation of slavery. Only a very small percentage of people in the South owned slaves, and few fought for the privilege of protecting others' rights to own slaves. Some felt that they were fighting for the rights of states to oppose an oppressive Federal government, but I maintain it was all about freedom and the right for them to live their life in a way that they determined.

However, that was all well and good, but the South could not accept their defeat. It is becoming increasingly evident that Democrats seem especially incapable of conceding to the consequences of not only losing elections but conflicts, for that matter. Lincoln had tried to make the union whole again by being very lenient to the southern states. Soldiers who fought for the confederacy, were allowed to take an oath of allegiance and return home with their horse and their firearms. President Johnson continued in that vein after Lincoln was assassinated but the South took advantage of his policies. To be more accurate, it was the Democrats who created the resistance that followed the war, because Democrats dominated Southern politics.

The Black Codes

Democrats tried to reestablish white supremacy-- through black codes that would keep slaves under control. The black codes dictated that all freedmen in the South had to register for employment. If they did not do so, they were classified as vagrants and had to pay a fine. Someone else could pay the fine but the black freedman was then indebted to that person and was required to make restitution through indentured servitude. It was just slavery draped in sheep's clothing.

It was the Democrats, who wanted to erase the consequences of losing a civil war, restore the status quo and pretend that it never happened. Johnson's southern bias resulted in his impeachment and it took a Republican Congress to place restrictions on the political power of Southern Democrats. In response, Democrat elements gave rise to the Ku Klux Klan and the terrorizing of Southern Blacks.

It was the Republicans who had to send the military to the South to enforce the laws and protect the freedmen. It was the Republicans who enacted the Thirteenth, Fourteenth, and Fifteenth Amendments which expanded legal rights and protections for Blacks. It was Democrats who resisted these measures at every turn. It was the

United Daughters of the Confederacy who became the propaganda arm of the Democrat party, by erecting statues to confederate heroes, controlling the narrative of history textbooks in southern schools and perpetrating the myth of the Lost Cause.

It was the Lost Cause that espoused the viewpoint that the South did nothing wrong and that they were justified in their actions. It was the Democrats who were the white supremacists. It was the Democrats who took their inspiration from one of the most racist movies ever made: The Birth of a Nation. It was Democrats who gave rise to a wave of lynching's that swept across the Southland. This is a legacy that continued with Jim Crow laws, and the racial segregation of the civil rights movement to the racism of present day.

AFTERMATH

Some contend that we have never fully healed and that we carry the scars to this day. That is the true legacy of the Civil War. Relations between the races have improved significantly over the last 150 years but we are still a long way from an equal and fully integrated society.

However, the civil war and its repercussions were significant in another respect. It is where the Democratic Party cut its teeth on many of the tactics that have succeeded in dividing this country and keeping it divided. George Orwell once stated that "Who controls the past, controls the future. Who controls the present controls the past." That is exactly what Southern Democrats realized long before Orwell came to write a single word.

Democrats began by not accepting the election of Abraham Lincoln in 1860. It was this election that triggered the secession of Southern states, the formation of the Confederacy and the outbreak of hostilities that led to the Civil War. After the war, the South was unable to accept its defeat and the consequences, most notably the freeing of the slaves. They could never accept that the slaves were human beings who were entitled to the same equal rights as they were. They resisted this concept at every turn. They tried to remain in power through every means possible because they knew that whoever had the power controlled the narrative.

They tried to erase history and pretend that the war never happened and that they had been defeated. They tried to replace history with their version so that they would influence how it was thought about and perceived in later years. For the most part they were successful. Despite their racist ancestry, they have become the party that champions the interests of Black people and it is Republicans who are characterized as racists. Amazing.

All of these leftist strategies, refusing to accept an outcome, resistance, erasing and rewriting history, perpetrating propaganda and indoctrinating our youth all had their genesis in these times. If this is a modus operandi that sounds familiar you are not alone. These are the same progenitors that are being employed today, the only difference is that with the advent of time, they have been perfected. Remember these schemes well because this is a discussion that we will revisit.

Many of the problems that haunt us today in our inner cities stem from not being able to adequately resolve issues that emanated from the Civil War. Knowing what we know why would we want to entertain, even for a minute, the thought of *ever* going down this road again? And yet I will tell you that all the harbingers indicate that it is preordained.

"Our safety, our liberty, depends upon preserving the Constitution of the United States as our fathers made it inviolate. The people of the United States are the rightful masters of both congress and the courts, not to overthrow the Constitution, but to overthrow the men who pervert the Constitution." Abraham Lincoln

THE LYNCHPIN

A thing that is critical to a system or organization.

The Constitution is the heart from which the rest of our institutions flow. This book primarily discusses three men, George Washington, Abraham Lincoln and Donald Trump and how they were the pivotal figures of their respective times. They were central figures in the preservation of the country during perilous times of civil unrest and war. They are truly deserving of the mantle American lynchpin. But men come and go. Our founders knew that.

And so, they provided the foundational lodestone that would transcend the mortality of a president. The Constitution is the Rosetta Stone that preserves our liberty across generations. It is the true American Lynchpin. But only if we respect it. It does have a flaw. It can be transformed or even ignored completely in the hands of those who would corrupt it.

Preamble to the Constitution:

We the people of the United States, in order to form a more perfect union, establish justice, insure domestic tranquility, provide for the common defense, promote the general welfare, and secure the blessings of liberty to ourselves and our posterity, do ordain and establish this Constitution for the United States of America.

Constitution of the United States (simplified version)

Article 1 – Creates the two parts of Congress. They are responsible for making laws.

Section 2

    A. Defines the House of Representatives, known as the lower house of Congress.

    B. Must be 25 years old, will serve for two years each. Must be a citizen 7 years.

    C. Each state gets Representatives based on state population.

    D. Has a leader called the Speaker of the House.

Section 3

    A. Defines the Senate, knows as the upper house of the Congress.

    B. Must be 30 years old, will serve for six years each. Must be a citizen 9 years.

    C. Each state gets two Senators.

    D. Vice-President breaks tie votes.

Section 4

    A. Says that each state may establish its own methods for electing members of the Congress.

    B. Requires, that Congress must meet at least once per year.

Section 5

    A. Says that Congress must have a minimum number of members present in order to meet.

    B. Fines for members who do not show up. It says that members may be expelled.

    C. Each house must keep a journal to record proceedings and votes.

    D. Neither house can adjourn without the permission of the other.

Section 6

    A. Establishes that members of Congress will be paid.

    B. They cannot be detained while traveling to and from Congress.

    C. That they cannot hold any other office in the government while in the Congress.

Section 7

    A. Say how bills become law.

    B. All bills must pass both houses of Congress in the exact same form.

    C. Bills that pass both houses are sent to the President.

    D. He can either sign the bill, in which case it becomes law, or he can veto it.

    E. If he vetoes a bill, it is sent back to Congress, and if both houses pass it by a two-thirds majority, the bill becomes law over the President's veto. This is known as overriding a veto.

Section 8

    A. Gives Congress the power to establish and maintain an army and navy.

    B. To establish post offices, to create courts, to regulate commerce between the states, to declare war, and to raise money.

Section 9

    A. Can not suspend right to remain silent laws.

    B. Can not pass laws that make things illegal starting yesterday or last week, etc.

    C. No law can give preference to one state over another

    D. Can not spend money without permission.

Section 10

    A. States can't make their own money, or declare war, or tax goods from other states.

Article 2 – Creates the job of President, called the Executive. Responsible for enforcing the laws.

Section 1

    A. Establishes the office of the President and the Vice-President.

    B. Both serve for four years.

    C. Presidents are elected by the Electoral.

    D. Must be 35 years old. Must be born in the USA.

    E. Their pay cannot change, up or down, as long as he in is office.

Section 2

    A. President leads the armed forces.

    B. He has a Cabinet to aid him, and can pardon criminals.

    C. He makes treaties with other nations (2/3 of the Senate have to approve of the treaty).

    D. Picks many of the judges and other members of the government.

Section 3

    A. President must give a yearly speech to the nation.

    B. Give suggestions to Congress.

    C. Meet with Ambassadors and other heads of state from other nations.

    D. Ensure the laws of the United States are carried out.

Section 4

    A. Explains how to kick the president from office, called impeachment.

Article 3 – Establishes Judges, called the Judiciary. They decide if a law is allowable, or if it goes against the Constitution.

Section 1

    A. Establishes the Supreme Court, the highest court in the United States.

    B. Judge serve for life, or until they want to retire.

Section 2

    A. Says what cases the Supreme Court must decide.

    B. It also guarantees trial by jury in criminal court.

Section 3

    A. Defines, without any question, what the crime of treason is.

Article 4 – States Rights.

Section 1

    A. All states will honor the laws of all other states.

Section 2

    A. Citizens of one state are treated equally and fairly like all citizens of another.

B. It also says that if a person accused of a crime in one state flees to another will be returned to the state that person fled from.

Section 3

A. How new states come into the Nation.
B. Control of federal lands.

Section 4

A. Ensures a "Power by the People" government.
B. Guarantees that the federal government will protect the states against.

Article 5 – How to change the Constitution.

A. 2/3 of the Representatives must vote on the change.
B. 2/3 of the Senators must vote on the change.
C. 3/4 of the States must vote for the change (34 or 50)

Article 6 – Concerns the United States.

A. Guarantees that the Constitution and all laws and treaties of the United States to be the supreme law of the country.
B. Requires all officers of the United States and of the states to swear an oath of allegiance to the United States and the Constitution when taking office.

Article 7 – Explained how the Constitution was agreed to.

A. Of the original 13 states in the United States, nine had to accept the Constitution before it would officially go into effect.

The Bill of Rights - Proposed in 1789 and enacted on December 15, 1791

1st Amendment

> Protects the people's right to practice religion, to speak freely, to assemble (meet), to address the government and of the press to publish.

2nd Amendment

> Protects the right to own guns.

3rd Amendment

> Guarantees that the army cannot force homeowners to give them room and board.

4th Amendment

> Protects the people from the government improperly taking property, papers, or people, without a valid warrant based on probable cause (good reason).

5th Amendment

> Protects people from being held for committing a crime unless they are properly indicted, that they may not be tried twice for the same crime, and that you need not be forced to testify against yourself. It also contains due process guarantees.

6th Amendment

> Guarantees a speedy trial, an impartial jury, and that the accused can confront witnesses against them, and that the accused must be allowed to have a lawyer.

7th Amendment

> Guarantees a jury trial in federal civil court cases. This type of case is normally no longer heard in federal court.

8th Amendment

> Guarantees that punishments will be fair, and not cruel, and that extraordinarily large fines will not be set.

9th Amendment

> Simply a statement that other rights aside from those listed may exist, and just because they are not listed doesn't mean they can be violated.

10th Amendment

> Says that any power not granted to the federal government belongs to the states.

Amendments passed once the Constitution was adopted.

11th Amendment - Enacted on February 7, 1795

> Says how someone from one state can sue another state.

12th Amendment - Enacted on June 15, 1804

> Redefines how the President and Vice-President are chosen by the Electoral College.

13th Amendment - Enacted on December 6, 1865

> Abolished slavery in the entire United States.

14th Amendment - Enacted on July 9, 1868

> People had rights on the federal level and on the state level, too. Dealt with civil war items.

15th Amendment - Enacted on February 3, 1870

> Ensured that a person's race could not be used as criteria for voting.

16th Amendment - Enacted on February 3, 1913

> Authorizes the United States to collect income taxes.

17th Amendment - Enacted on April 8, 1913

> Shifted the choosing of Senators from the state legislatures to the people of the states.

18th Amendment - Enacted on January 16, 1919

> Abolished the sale or manufacture of alcohol in the United States.

19th Amendment - Enacted on August 18, 1920

> Ensures that sex could not be used as a criteria for voting.

20th Amendment - Enacted on January 23, 1933

>Set new start dates for the terms of the Congress and the President.

21st Amendment - Enacted on December 5, 1933

>Repealed the 18th Amendment.

22nd Amendment - Enacted on February 27, 1951

>Set a limit on the number of times a President could be elected - two four-year terms.

23rd Amendment - Enacted on March 29, 1961

>Grants the Washington D.C. the right to three electors in Presidential elections.

24th Amendment - Enacted on January 23, 1964

>Ensured that no tax could be charged to vote for any federal office.

25th Amendment - Enacted on February 10, 1967

>Establishes rules for a President who becomes unable to perform his duties while in office.

26th Amendment - Enacted on July 1, 1971

>Ensures that any person 18 or over may vote.

27th Amendment - Enacted on May 7, 1992

Any law that increased the pay of legislators may not take effect until after an election.

Simplified version by Aaron T. Larson

It took six thousand years of humanity to produce the documents of the Constitution." Neil Gorsuch 12/16 19 Fox and Friends

The Constitut`ion was a system of enumerated checks and balances to restrict the acquisition of power by any single entity. It was designed to prevent a monarchy. Its fault, that even the founders acknowledged, is that its effectiveness is limited by the quality of the people in the government who live under it. The Constitution is predicated by the assumption that 'good' people will 'honor' it.

"A Republic,… if you can keep it".

Benjamin Franklin

PART II

Disclaimer: Dear reader; please be advised that you enter this phase of the book at your own risk. Any resemblance to tactics and schemes presently employed by leftists, liberals and Democrats is not purely a coincidence--it is intentional.

> "If you tell a lie big enough and keep repeating it, people will eventually come to believe it."
>
> Joseph Goebbels

By all rights we should all be speaking German to each other. Germany was the single most powerful military nation in the world during WWII and could have defeated any other nation in a head to head conflict including the United States. But they took on too many nations at the same time and this was ultimately their downfall.

When Hitler and the Nazis took over Germany in 1932, they recognized that in order to solidify their power it was vital that they control crucial elements of society. One of the elements was the media and another was education. It was what the Nazi's referred to as "synchronization". There is a great parallel to what is happening in America today. It is a pattern of operation that we will see played out over and over again. It is almost as if the left has stolen the playbook of Nazi Germany and employed it for their purposes and yet they are the ones who resort to calling President Trump a Nazi.

The strategy of the left and the Nazis was similar in that they were both designed to control the population in order to perpetuate their power. Control of the majority equals power. I submit that the left has perfected this manipulation by masterfully coordinating the two elements, so they dovetail together like hand in glove. The difference is that the Nazis were nationals who wanted to restore Germany to international prominence. The left wants to use their power to reduce America's presence on the world stage and we will get into this matter in more detail in another chapter. But as proof of this, one only has to look no further than Barack Obama and his apology tour, just after he was elected when he went around the world apologizing for the evil that America had inflicted on all the other countries of the world.

However, before the left began employing these techniques, there were the Nazis and they were some of the most evil architects the world has ever known.

STATE OF EDUCATION IN NAZI GERMANY

The Nazis were quick to recognize that the schools held the future of Germany. Moreover, they were the future of his ideology and so Hitler viewed them as the training grounds and recruitment centers for his purposes. He knew that he was going to need an army and they were his future soldiers. The purpose of the schools in the Hitlerian scheme of things was to indoctrinate students into the racial ideas of the Nazi party and to extract a personal allegiance to the Fuhrer. Aryan mothers were conditioned to further the pure Aryan race and prepare their sons to be loyal soldiers.

The tools of purge and replace were the first steps in the takeover of the education system. All Jewish teachers were fired. A Nazi teacher's association was created in order to screen teachers for their racial and political compatibilities. A teacher was required to become a member and compliance was close to 100%.

Teachers were trained in the Nazi ideology. If they did not teach the Nazi ideology in an effective manner in the classroom, the pupils could report their teachers to the authorities. Now there's a novel concept. If the teachers in our current system could be put on report for being ineffective educators, we would have a lot of empty classrooms.

There was an incident of a German teacher who grew weary of the regimentation that was imposed on the learning process. He implored his students to just have a conversation with him, like normal human beings and not like "programmed robots and automatons". He was reported to the authorities and sent to a concentration camp. My, my, how evolved and civilized we have become since then. In America or at least New York City, if a teacher is put on report, they are sent to a Rubber Room (a kind of detention room for teachers on suspension).

Textbooks that did not exemplify the Nazi's vison of German greatness, were thrown into huge bonfires and the Nazi controlled press began rewriting the new version of events. That's the protocol. Once you purge, you have to follow up and replace it.

That includes the curriculum. Religious education was banned. That sounds vaguely familiar. Eugenics replaced religion. Physical education was emphasized in place of some of the sciences built on reason and logic. Hitler had enough scientists--what he needed was obedient soldiers. It is eerily similar to what the schools of today are turning out--soldiers for the leftist cause. The German version of the boy scouts at that time was taken over by the Hitler Youth which was essentially a more targeted and accelerated military training program.

The Nazi domination of the education system would ensure obeisance to the Nazi ideals for generations and the result was a soulless, mindless automaton who would be complicit in the murder of six million Jews. It explains how the Holocaust was made possible.

A mindless, soulless, sycophant has similarities to what is occurring in American schools and society today. This is the same blueprint that the leftists are following.

This is where the Democrats learned to perfect their strategies.

STATE OF THE MEDIA IN NAZI GERMANY

Propaganda is information that is utilized to persuade an audience to accept a certain ideology or cause. The method is to perpetrate a 'truth' based on biased or false material or by appealing to emotions rather than reason. It was the seminal instrument in the Nazis rise to power in 1930 Germany. It was the predicate, accompanied by a campaign of purge and replace. Another scheme adopted in more recent times by American left-wingers.

The day Hitler became Chancellor in 1933 was the day any semblance of democracy died in Germany. All opposition political parties were abolished. Germany was transformed almost overnight into a totalitarian state. A law was passed that prohibited any ethnic group, except Aryan, to be an editor or publisher of a newspaper. When Hitler took power there were around 4700 newspapers in operation and by the end of the Third Reich only about a thousand were left, all under state control and all pro-Nazi.

"The Propaganda Ministry aimed further to control the content of the news and editorial pages through directives distributed in daily conferences in Berlin and transmitted via the Nazi Party propaganda offices to regional or local papers. Detailed guidelines stated what stories could or could not be reported and how to report the news."

Holocaust Encyclopedia.

The object of the Nazi propaganda machine was two- fold--to promote anti-Semitism and to create a narrative of Aryan supremacy. Only points of view that were in accordance with these two themes were permitted.

"The broad masses of the people are not... persons who are able to form reasoned judgement, in given cases, but a vacillating crowd of human children who are constantly wavering between one idea and another...that its thought and conduct are ruled by sentiment than by sober reasoning." (Mien Kampf)

Joseph Goebbels was appointed Minister of Propaganda and his first undertaking was to identify all the books and written materials in libraries and in schools that were considered non-conforming to Nazi ideology. These materials were gathered together in ostentatious demonstrations at night and burned at rallies around bonfires. The purging stage had begun. Once all dissenting opinions and oppositional materials had been expunged from the intellectual forum, the way was clear for replacement. Goebbels was a master at instilling the Nazi ideology into the minds of the German citizens. New books and articles were written, espousing only the Nazi point of view. Newspapers extolled only Nazi virtues and successes.

Goebbels campaign for the heart minds and soul of the German populace was in full gear. Actually, it was a page taken right out of Hitler's Mein Kampf and it was more like an assault of the "repeated exposure effect". (Goebbels)

The following quotes give us an idea of how and why they were able to perpetrate their schemes on the unsuspecting masses.

"Propaganda must not investigate the truth objectively..., yet it must present only that aspect of the truth which is favorable to its own side." (Mein Kampf)

"To deprive its objects of the power of independent thought." (Albert Speer)

"To absorb the individual into a mass of like-minded people." (Neil Gregor, historian)

"Another core part of the Nazi grand theory was the dethronement of reason and celebration of emotion."

"The ability to see into the soul of the people and to speak the language of the man in the street." (Goebbels)

Textbooks for schools were Nazi revisionist versions of history. Mein Kampf became required reading for the German population. It was Hitler's treatise on the future of Germany, written while he was in prison. It sold few copies until after he was elected and then sales skyrocketed and made him a millionaire. It was his personal blueprint for ruling Germany.

Goebbels was not content to stop there but brought the full weight of communication technology to bear, in the form of radio and films. He implemented a program of government subsidy that enabled 70% of the German population to purchase a radio. And since it was the Nazis who controlled the airwaves, it proved to be a direct pipeline of their propaganda into the average German household. Not unlike the pipeline of propaganda from CNN and MSNBC.

Goebbels recruited the likes of Leni Riefenstahl, who was a genius at making movies that portrayed Hitler in a deity-like image and she excelled in the glorification of Nazi spectacles. The Jewish people on the other hand, were demonized and dehumanized, as justification for the horrific treatment that the Nazis were inflicting on them.

The purpose of all this was to create a huge segment of the population that would be 'all in' regarding their allegiance to Hitler and the Nazis and they would follow him without question to the ends of the earth. And that they did exactly that--right off the cliff to near total destruction.

In the process they took along 60 million others in a conflagration that engulfed the rest of the world. That's the beautiful thing about propaganda--it creates a bubble that is not based on truth and everyone that gets sucks into the bubble believes it, until they are all living in a fantasy land telling each other the lies that they all want to hear.

Even when the German army was near destruction and the Russian and American armies were knocking at the ruined doorstep of Berlin, Hitler and Goebbels were still telling the German people that they were on the verge of victory. As the whole crazy merry-go-round was spinning off its axis and into the canyon, the majority of the German people were still on board, hanging on with both hands.

The betrayal of truth to the American people by the mainstream media that was supposedly founded on the very principle of truth-seeking, is the biggest lie ever perpetrated on the citizens of this country. Our fourth estate has become our fifth column.

I submit that because of this failure and the other parallels to the American education system, that will become evident, we are practically witnessing the rebirth of Nazi Germany. It is truly chilling.

THE STATE OF EDUCATION IN AMERICA

"The philosophy of the schoolroom in one generation is the philosophy of government in the next." (Abraham Lincoln)

"We don't need no education
We don't need no thought control
No dark sarcasm in the classroom
Teachers leave them kids alone
Hey, teachers, leave them kids alone
All in all its just another brick in the wall
All in all you're just another brick in the wall"
'Another Brick in the Wall' song by Pink Floyd

Liberals were smart enough to recognize the importance of exercising control over our youth. The liberal movement in the school system started in the colleges with protesters over the Vietnam War. Student and professors joined in expressing their dissatisfaction with the American government. As radical and left leaning students graduated, they got jobs as professors and teachers and over time they not only infiltrated colleges but the public schools as well. Once they had sufficient control over the key components of the school environment and the school boards, they were able to put in place their campaign to indoctrinate students, according to their liberal values and agendas.

As they graduate more students who also become teachers for the cause, the system perpetuates itself and ultimately conservatives are squeezed out. I found it outrageous that as a conservative educator, I was essentially mandated to join the teacher's union and my dues were used to make campaign contributions to Democratic candidates--people I would never vote for in a million years.

Presently all aspects of our schools are dominated by liberals and our country has become the product of that liberal cultivation. Liberals are beginning to reap what they have sowed. That may have been the biggest mistake the conservative movement in this country has made-- underestimating the impact of influence in our education system and surrendering it so easily to the liberals. In my opinion we will pay a huge price for this miscalculation as we will see later, because it is fundamentally changing our society and the way it thinks.

One of the hardest parts of writing this book, for me, was having to include the section on the state of our education system in this country. It was as if in the writing of this book I had to relive the crime all over again. I was a public-school educator for the last fifteen years of my working career and I was a frontline witness to the destruction it did to our children. Truth be told, I was more than a witness, I was an unwitting accomplice and it broke my heart almost daily, once I realized what was happening.

You must understand something. There is a realization to be grasped here. And once you recognize that realization, a light will come on and everything will begin to make sense. You will see how all the pieces fit together into one giant puzzle and only then will it all make perfect sense. And it all begins with the education system.

That realization didn't happen for me right away. Call me naïve and I guess that's what I was, but I think I can be forgiven this fault given the circumstances. Before I reveal my epiphany let me take you on a little journey that might explain how I happened on this discovery.

I was a career changer and had worked in the private sector for thirty years before I got into teaching. In the private sector, I was used to getting results--it was how you kept your job, it was how you got raises, it was how you got promoted, it was how success was measured. The reason that I got into teaching was that I thought I would be good at getting students to learn. I felt that I had gotten a solid education when I was in grade school and it had served me fairly well throughout my life. I thought that it would be a platform for an effective career as an educator. All of my life I loved to learn about new things and that was fueled by a love of reading. I was fortunate to have been encouraged to read from an early age. In many of my early grades, students were given prizes by the number of books that they read and reviewed, in the course of the school year. I think I would have been an avid reader even if it hadn't been incentivized because I enjoyed it. I also had a model.

My father also supported my reading and was the perfect role model. This from a man who never made it past the sixth grade and yet he could carry an intelligent conversation, on almost any subject with anybody. He was a man who had a veracious appetite for learning.

He was forced to drop out of school to go to work to help his family survive the depression. Then came World War II, where he served as a tail gunner in twenty missions over Europe. Having survived the war, he returned home and could have gone to school on the GI bill but chose to get married and start a family. With a family to support, he forsook a chance at education to work in a steel mill. He spent the rest of his life there and hated almost every minute of it.

But every Saturday (with me in tow when I was younger) he went to the library and checked out at least 10 books to read and finished them all before the next Saturday. And he did that every week of his life. The result was that he was one of the smartest men that I ever knew. And he was adamant that his kids get an education above everything else. (Of course, that was a time long, long ago and far, far away when parents trusted schools to educate their children.)

He was so dedicated to that proposition that after I graduated from high school, I was seriously considering foregoing college (even though I had secured an athletic scholarship) and following in his footsteps as a steel worker. In fact, I started working in the steel mill that summer but when fall came I was mysteriously fired from my job. With few options available I decided to attend college and it was a decision that profoundly transformed my life.

I can promise you with the highest degree of certainty that had I not gone down *that* path, I would not be in any position to be sitting here writing this book. I would not have had the skills, the life experiences or the opportunities required for writing and producing a work of this nature. It wasn't until many years later, that I learned that my father had persuaded the foreman to fire me because he knew in his infinite wisdom, that I would never have been satisfied with his lot in life as a steelworker.

My father passed away before I got my doctorate and even though I know he would have been proud of that accomplishment, I was never as educated as my father, who never got past the 6th grade. It was because he read more than I ever did, and he was self-educated. To this day I have never met anyone who read as much as he did.

But then, I never met Abraham Lincoln. It is the contention of this book that Abraham Lincoln was the American Lynchpin of the Civil War and he too was a totally self-educated man.

"All I have learned, I learned from books." (Abraham Lincoln)

Anyway, with my background as a basis, I thought that I would be good at inspiring young students to learn and that's why I became a teacher. Perhaps I was naïve in my idealism. Imagine someone getting into a profession with the idea that maybe they could make other lives better. In teacher speak, everyone repeats the same mantra; "They just wanted to make a difference".

I had no illusions that I was "born" to be a teacher. I certainly wasn't. But I wanted to give it a try and so I applied to an organization, Urban Teachers of America/Teach America that specialized in recruiting prospective teachers to fill areas of high need. 'Areas of high need' could be defined as a subject matter that was experiencing a shortage of qualified educators, or a segment of the school population such as special education. It could also mean in a school in an area of the country where no one wanted to teach, such as an inner-city location with a Title I designation.

Title I means that the school is eligible for a subsidized lunch program which usually translates into a very poor neighborhood. A primary goal of the Teach America organization (which lent to my deception) was that they were trying to improve the quality of education by attempting to break the cycle of incompetence. The theory was that undesirable areas or subject matters attract the worst teachers and those teachers turn out less educated students who in turn become teachers in the same underprivileged neighborhoods. Thus, the poor quality of education is perpetuated like a self-fulfilling prophecy.

When I was teaching, I would see evidence of this constantly. Whenever I walked into an English classroom in the school that I was assigned to, I would find the writing on the blackboard (written by the teacher) covered in spelling and grammatical errors. This would have been unimaginable in my grade school classroom as a youth.

The intention of a group like Teach America was to infuse areas identified as deficient, with new blood (usually from outside) that had the necessary skills and qualifications to raise the overall standards of education, in that particular area or school. They did that by offering idealism, incentives and requiring that their recruits commit to a contract of a certain number of years.

It was kind of like the Peace Corps meets enlistment in the armed forces, only with benefits. I must have hit the trifecta on the disadvantaged spectrum--as I was assigned to teach science(a subject nobody wanted to teach anymore) to special education students(a population no one wanted to be associated with) in a minority neighborhood(that looked more like a war zone) in the Bronx, New York(where no one wanted to go).

Then the games began. The first thing I noticed that was different from the private sector was that everything in the field of education is couched in an acronym. Every industry employs acronyms to a certain extent, but I have never been in a field of employment that uses so many acronyms, that it is like they are all talking in a foreign language.

I think it is a veteran of the system's way of either intimidating or impressing a newcomer with their insider knowledge. It signals to the neophyte that "Hey I'm no tenderfoot, I'm a member of the club." If only they thought it was as important to express their knowledge of their subject matter. But then that would only expose how unknowledgeable they really are.

"Better to remain silent and be thought a fool than to speak and remove all doubt." (attributed to Abraham Lincoln)

The second thing I noticed about educators was the metrics of the system. In the private sector employee success was measured by results. In education, employee success is measured by longevity. For every year that you participate in the system, the higher you are paid, which in turn directly drives your retirement. The pay scale is written right into the teacher contract and you know exactly what you will earn in any given year that is covered by the contract.

And that is *regardless* of your performance as a teacher.

In this system, you don't have to be good at your job, you just have to be good at hanging around.

The only time that performance seems to be of any significance is when you are trying to get tenure. Tenure (for those unfamiliar with the system) is kind of like an apprenticeship, in the first few years of a new teacher. In that period of time, if a school or a principal decides that for any reason you are not a good fit, they can terminate you unconditionally.

On the other hand, if they decide that they want to retain you, they will grant you tenure and that is essentially the golden ticket that entitles the teacher to a job for life. After achieving tenure, teacher performance is almost inconsequential to job retention, unless you do something egregious--like sexual misconduct or something of that nature.

The only value that I ever saw in tenure is that it protected teachers, in the event that they worked for a vindictive principal, who just wanted to get rid of teachers because of personal dislike. Principals in New York City are afforded an inordinate amount of power over all aspects of their school, but at least their power was somewhat restricted when it concerned a teacher who had attained tenure. Especially when it concerned a teacher who was a conservative.

Tenure was a good thing when it concerned a good teacher and a bad principal because it afforded that teacher some security, but it worked to the detriment of the students when you have a good principal and a bad teacher. The latter is a lot more common than the former, and it is reflected in the poor state of affairs of the education system and its protectionist union.

Tenure is probably one of the worst concepts in a system that is predicated on seniority. The end result is that it rewards mediocrity and perpetuates incompetence. That and the teacher's unions who perpetrate the complete hoax--that they care about the education of our children--are the worst indictments of our education system.

The only thing the teacher unions care about is remaining in power so that they can control the whole system, even if it is failing our students. If teacher unions really cared about the welfare of our children, they would not be so strenuously opposed to charter schools, when in almost every instance, charter schools are outperforming their public- school counterparts.

In minority school districts parents of Black and Hispanic students are on their hands and knees pleading for school choice and are being denied that option by the teacher unions and the political influence they command. Their children are hopelessly trapped in these failing schools and they know it. Is that how the union shows it concern for students?

They have even gone so far as to close down charter schools that had proven successful track records. How good was that for the students who benefitted from being in those schools? Don't be fooled by the teacher unions. They don't care about your kids. And that is your first lesson. That was my first realization. But that is just the beginning.

It gets worse.

A lot worse.

The New York Department of Education, in their infinite wisdom, designated me as a science teacher. It was at this point that I began to wonder about the judgement of my employers. I didn't even have a certification to teach science, but I was told not to worry, because it would be covered under the umbrella of my special education license. I guess that covered the legality of the situation, but I was worried about something else, that I considered of far more importance.

I didn't have any knowledge of science.

The last time I had even been in a science class was in high school and that was over 30 years ago.

I had no training as a science teacher and for that matter, no teacher training whatsoever from the New York City Department of Education (NYCDOE). That didn't seem to bother anybody, except me. Leave it up to the NYCDOE to not let a little detail like that get in the way. I was told that the science opening was where they had the need and that was the position available and if I wanted to teach, I would either have to take it or leave it. I did want to teach so I took it.

The book that follows this one describes my experiences as an educator in more detail, so I have deferred to a passage from that work.

Excerpt from "A Special Kind of Stupid: The Persecution of an American Educator."

Now not only was I being exposed to diversity in the extreme (for the first time in my life I was a minority in the most dramatic sense) but I was expected to teach these students. Teach them...I had no understanding of what they were about. I had always been under the impression that in order to teach something, you had to have an understanding of your subject and your audience. I certainly had no understanding of my audience. By the way, in case I haven't mentioned it, I had been hired to teach science--a subject for which I had no license or certification. It was a content area in which I had not taken a course since high school some 30 years ago-- but apparently it was a situation in which the New York City Department of Education, in its infinite wisdom, deemed me eminently qualified.

That was only the first problem in a host of other problems.

Least of which was that I had no textbooks or course materials. Another situation in which the NYCDOE didn't seem overly concerned about. In fact, there was not a stitch of instructive material in the entire classroom including the walls and shelves of this third-floor hothouse. There I was on the third floor of a brick building that had no air conditioning, save for an ancient electric fan in the corner that looked like it was a refugee from a hotel lobby from the nineteen-forties.

While I didn't know anything about science my math training certainly came in handy. I soon learned that the way to calculate the temperature in your room was to take the outside temperature and add 10° for each floor that you went up. So, for instance if it was 80° outside, the second floor would be 90 and the third floor would be 100°-- especially in afternoons when the sun came through our windows and baked us like worms under a magnifying glass. Under those conditions it was hard to do anything else but sit there and watch each other sweat.

I was quickly beginning to see why so many teachers washed out in the first few years of this profession. It's no wonder that in this kind of brutal environment, 50% of teachers quit during their first year in teaching, 75% are gone by second year and by the fifth year only 10% of teachers remain in the profession. It seemed that the approach of the school and the DOE was to provide new teachers with the worst possible conditions and see who survived. We did not get our textbooks until a couple months into the school year. At the time I figured that this must be some strange rite of passage for new teachers. It was almost a designed trial-by-fire. But that would be an assumption that gives the DOE too much credit. I can be forgiven because I still had a lot to learn. The truth of the matter is that the only thing the education department ever plans is gross incompetence and failure.

I personally don't agree with this approach, whether by design or accident and I think the system would be better served by providing more support to new teachers but strange as it may seem, this strategy actually worked with me and it made me a better teacher today. At the time, though, I was doing anything I could just to survive. Even the janitors had a betting pool against how long I would last. And the long money had me out by the *end* of the week. Even I had to concede the overly optimistic folly of that wager.

There's an old adage that sailors recite when they are caught in a storm and the ship is in extreme peril. I found it applied to this situation perfectly. They talk about when 'the waves turn the minutes to hours'. That had to be the longest week of my life. Every time I looked at the clock it seemed to be running backward.

Imagine yourself in front of 35 minority kids whose culture you didn't understand, who had no use for education and didn't want to be there, in a room that was 100 degrees, with no educational materials of any kind. I did everything I could think of—told stories, asked questions, led the class in physical exercises, brought in newspapers for current events. One day we found an ancient computer and printer, in pieces, in one of the closets.

This might have been the first computer that Adam and Eve ever used, but I didn't care. My previous background was in high-tech and I knew a little bit about hardware and software and so the class project became to put this computer back together.

At that point I didn't care if it worked or not--just trying to put it back together would be enough to keep the class occupied, at least for a while. After all this was science class. The bonus, to the astonishment of all of us, most of all myself, was that once we had it assembled, not only did the computer work but the printer printed. It was astounding that aside from computers in the administrative offices, we had the only other working computer in the entire school.

I never knew at the time what a boon this would prove to be for my situation. There was nothing that these kids, poor as they were, related to more than technology. When you came right down to it, they were actually quite computer savvy and so, not only could we use the computer for researching and learning about content, but it was a great incentive. Students earned the privilege to go on it, when they had completed their regular lessons. It was nothing less than a Godsend and truth be told, (although I never told the janitors this) it literally saved my teaching career.

I learned early on how technology could be incorporated into the classroom and if used properly, what a tool it could be to enhance student engagement and academic performance. That was a lifesaver and I had my technical expertise in my previous life to thank for it. That's how I survived my first week."

But if I didn't know better (and here I will use a term from my previous tenure in the private sector) I was beginning to get the suspicion that I was being "set up to fail."

I wondered about other things.

Let me start off by saying, that in my opinion students today are getting the short end of the stick by our public education system. Many of the teachers I witnessed had no skills to be in front of a classroom.

A perfect example was a science teacher, who I was assigned to assist in an inclusion class. What that meant was that she was assigned a regular education class of say, twenty-five students but also six special education students. However, the six special education students had to be accompanied by a special education teacher, (which was me) to assist them with help they may need, answer questions and support them with any extra guidance that they might require.

I always thought science was one of the best subjects to teach learning challenged students because a teacher could make it interactive and hands-on with the number of experiments you could do. Apparently, this teacher held an entirely different view of teaching science. Her method was to pull out the science textbook (which we were finally supplied) and begin reading word for word from the text. She never took any questions. She barely made eye contact with the students in the class until she was done reading.

Then there were questions in the textbook at the end of each chapter and she would assign these for the students to work on. Every day was the same routine for 90 minutes twice a week. This was her class, she was in charge, I had no say in how it was conducted, and not once did she ask me for any input. I can tell you the students who I was assigned to assist, abhorred every minute of this teacher's instruction and I could not blame them. Even for me as a teacher, this was the most mind-numbing exhibition of learning I had ever witnessed.

There was no element of teaching that I could discern from this method. She just read from the textbook and did not deviate one iota. Why not just assign the chapter for the students to read themselves? She obviously equated her reading of the chapter verbatim, with the skill of teaching. There were students that would have preferred jumping out of the window, rather than endure another 90-minute session with her. Fortunately, we were on the ground floor so it would not have had the desired effect.

Naturally student behavior in the class escalated and by the end of the year, most of the students had been kicked out of the class. Students who should have been in a classroom that was exposing them to the principles of science, were sitting in detention hall because of a teacher who did not have a clue how to present an engaging lesson. The sad part is that the kids in detention hall, were getting just as good an education as the kids in the science class itself--none.

And yet to my complete and utter astonishment, the administration loved this teacher. She was always right on schedule with the track of her curriculum and her grades and paperwork were always current and delivered on time. At faculty meetings she was always getting praise from the principal and presented as an example for the rest of us to follow. I could not believe *this* was the example that the education system held in high regard. There was no real learning going on in that classroom and the administrators were perfectly fine with that.

I am sure that this teacher had a long and successful career in education and not one of her students ever learned a damn thing in her class. The only way a teacher of this nature could even hold her job, never mind thrive, is because of the teacher unions and the climate in the school systems. Our children are captive audiences in these horrendous learning environments and is it any wonder that they are graduating without any discernible skills?

You better hang onto your hats because they are about to be blown away. It's a foul wind that blows through the hallways of our schools nowadays.

In contrast, I found myself in a situation that I deemed inexplicable. I was being mentored at the time by an organization called Telling America's Story. I mentioned earlier in this book about "Forgotten Patriots" a story about Revolutionary War prisoners who died on prison ships, rather than swear allegiance to the crown of England.

On this particular day we were studying that book. It had just been released and was hailed by the historical community as cutting-edge material. There were copies of the book available to us educators as well as an instructional DVD. Edwin Burrows, the author, came to speak about his book to our group. It was an impressive presentation. As a result, I worked up a lesson plan on the subject matter based on the materials I had been given.

I was so excited that I was going to be able to deliver such an exciting, ground-breaking lesson to my class. But first I had to have the lesson plan approved by the principal's office. However, since there was no mention of the patriots held as prisoners in the textbook we were using, I was prohibited from delivering the lesson. It was one of the greatest episodes of American patriotism and it was not going to be permitted because it was not in some textbook that was probably ten years old. I was beside myself to say the least. From this experience I learned that the textbook was regarded as the Holy Grail of all instruction. You know the one. The textbook that new teachers don't get issued until the year is almost half over. Yea that's the one.

On some of the cable news shows that I watch, reporters go out into the streets and ask questions of ordinary passers-by. There are all different generations represented in these 'man-in-the-street' interviews but generally the majority of respondents come from the younger generations such as genXers and millennials. They appear to be college graduates in their mid-twenties, now out in the working world.

One of the questions was "Who fought in the Civil War?" This is a pretty straight forward question in my opinion and only requires a basic knowledge of American history. Very few got it right. The other answers were embarrassing and ranged from foreign countries to foreign continents.

Another question on Thanksgiving Day was "Who was at the first Thanksgiving." I was stunned at the answers that were given. One person said that he believed "that there were some people from Sweden." Someone else who was trying to be cute in their attempt to display their obvious expertise on the subject and responded in this manner, "In nineteen hundred and forty-two, Columbus sailed the ocean blue." No, what you just read was not a misprint. This person was beaming proudly as if they had just recited the Gettysburg Address from memory.

In another instance, when the reporter asked the question, the person stated immediately that they had no clue. The reporter tried to help out and actually give a clue and said "It was the Pil…."

When the person in the street heard the first three letters her eyes lit up with that lightbulb that goes on in your head when you think you've just recognized what the answer is. Then just as quickly the light went out and the response was, "I don't have a clue."

What is so sad about this is that these are young adults who are out in the working world and have been in the public-school system for as many as 12 or 13 years. This is what we are graduating. This is our finished product. These are the future leaders of our country.

My question is "What are we doing with those 13 years if we are not even teaching the rudiments of a basic education? Unfortunately, having been in the system for 15 years, I know what the answer is.

Our schools don't care about educating our children.

In fact, the converse is true. If we truly cared about education in this country, we would demand some sort of accountability. When a college graduate cannot identify who was at the first Thanksgiving, every social studies teacher that that student ever had from grade school to college should be summarily fired. It is disgraceful what our schools are turning out. A current study of a comparison of students from other countries found that Asian students are 4 grade levels above American students.

"This is one of the most damning indictments of our education system that I have ever come across, and it is yet another clear indication that what we are doing is simply not working. Our children are not being given the tools that they need to compete in our modern society and we have only ourselves to blame." (End of the American Dream 12/4/2019 by Michael Snyder)

But more on this in the next section.

Having spent 15 years in the education system as a teacher, special education case manager and mental health counsellor, it has always been a theory of mine that the system, even though they claimed to the contrary, never wanted to graduate kids who could think for themselves. In fact, I always believed that the exact opposite was the goal of the people (liberals) in charge of the education system in our country. Now some of you may be shocked at this statement but let me try to explain further by using examples from my career in teaching.

I was a career changer when I got into education. I really regretted that I had not gotten into it sooner, as I really loved it and it always felt that I had found my niche in life. I always said, that I loved the job, but I despised the system. I was always guided by the precept that I knew my students were not going to remember all the names and dates that would be covered in the course of a year and that was to be expected. However, if they came away with anything from being in my class, it was the ability to think critically. I did not want to give them a fish, I wanted to teach them how to fish, so they could feed themselves for the rest of their lives. But unfortunately, this runs exceedingly counter to the objectives of the education system. Their prime directive is not to teach students *how* to think but *what* to think.

There are a lot of "bad" teachers in the education system just like the one that was described earlier, who recited her textbook. Most have never been properly trained (and I contend that is by design) others are lazy, and some are just incompetent. The teacher unions perpetrate the whole failing system.

"Government unions have politicized and polarized our teachers-on purpose-by silencing the voices and values of teachers and parents...I learned that damaging undertow my very first month as a student teacher. We can debate, deliberate and assign 'experts' to the issues and rob another fifty years' worth of students of their best hope at success, or we can start listening to the real experts-parents and teachers-and win our schools and country back." (Rebecca Friederichs, "Standing up to Goliath")

As a result, our kids are trapped in this "another brick in the wall" environment. Outside of school, everything around them is telling these students that education has no relevance to their lives. Theirs is a tough life on the streets with poverty, violence, guns, knives, drugs and death. Where does education fit into that scenario? When they do get in the school, the thinking that school has nothing to offer them is only reinforced by an authoritarian environment of boring teachers, using uninspiring methods to promote conformity. And all that is acerbated by mental, emotional, and learning disorders such as ADHD, autism etc. that create a learning space that is volatile at best.

It's an atmosphere where a physical confrontation can result in fists flying and desks being overturned at any time, where cursing is commonplace, where bars on windows is normal and where kids who can't commit suicide by jumping through an upper floor window will resort to throwing themselves down a stairwell instead. It's a place where kids are just as likely to be taken out of school in handcuffs or in a straight- jacket. It is no wonder that kids see school as a place that has nothing to offer them.

I always considered it a blessing that I was recruited to teach science, even though as I mentioned before, that I had no degree or even a license to teach that particular subject. Nevertheless, I went into it, full bore. I inherited a classroom that had nothing in it but bare shelves. That didn't last long. I used my own money to buy anything I could get my hands on. Supplies for experiments, games, art supplies, rockets, computer supplies, robotics and even various assorted animals, hamsters, birds, fish, ants and crabs.

I enrolled in the 'Globe Science Initiative' and earned classroom supplies through my participation with that organization. My intent was to turn those four bare walls into a living 'learn-atorium,' even though I was advised against it by my much more experienced colleagues, who said that it was a waste of time and money.

They said that these kids would never learn anyway, and in the end, since they had no respect for school, they would probably destroy everything in the room anyway. I thought that I would give it a shot, regardless of what they said. There was no question that I was the rookie, but in this case, I wanted to trust my instincts and if it was the wrong thing to do, then at least I wanted to be proven wrong.

That became the day I learned never to listen to the already jaded, creative-thought-challenged, teacher union subsidized, veterans of the status quo.

Longevity does not equate to excellence in the classroom and probably denotes just the opposite. Because what happened in my science room was just the opposite of what they had predicted.

The kids adopted the animals in my room as if they were their own pets. They came in early before class to feed them and play with them. Instead of abusing the animals, they bonded in their respect for them and that expanded to include each other, something that might not have been there previously. I had LESS problems after I decided to go with this approach, even though I was in a position that was more vulnerable to misconduct. The potential for disaster was certainly in place.

Maybe it was because I had placed a lot of trust in the conduct of the students and they recognized that. For once they weren't being dictated to and they responded with kindness. In my room, they saw a reason to *come* to school. In fact, it was interesting, that for kids who were so dead set against school, all I had to say was that if there was misconduct, they would *not* be allowed further access to the animals. To them, the exclusion that they had previously so desired, all of a sudden became a punishment.

I felt that this science room was an incubator of creativity, contrary to the regimental structure and the suffocating, suppressive attitude that was prevalent throughout the rest of the school. I am of the opinion, that creativity is on the highest level of a hierarchy that combines freedom and self- actualization. I think it was what the framers had in mind when they cast the phrase "pursuit of happiness", which is a direct result of having the freedom to be creative.

It was one of the reasons that I found teaching to be so fulfilling. There are always certain constraints in education that you cannot escape, but even within those confines, I often found myself in position to have great freedom to design and create a lesson of my own imagination. And to see it work as planned, and have the desired outcome, was the ultimate satisfaction.

This science room was that kind of island of creativity for these kids. And it became more so when I used it for the basis of my 'Hands-on Science' afterschool program. The first semester that I offered it, I only had two or three students enroll. It is amazing how word of mouth is transformative. By the second year, I had full enrollment and the program had to turn away students because of lack of room. The program director told me that my class was the most requested activity in the entire program.

I attribute that to the "trigger" theory. We had something of interest for everyone and we had no rules, other than to respect the property and their classmates. These kids were free to create their own experience. We did so many things. We made colored 'slime' and sold it to raise money for school activities. We built and shot rockets in the school yard. We brought in all kinds of objects like printers and televisions and deconstructed them to see how they worked. You can't believe how educational and fun it is to take something apart.

We were flying high. The kids were learning and enjoying themselves doing it, which is really the "dirty" little secret of education. If you can "disguise" learning in the "cloak" of a fun activity, you can "trick" your students into learning without them knowing it. We were learning, having fun and getting along as a group, with almost non-existent behavioral problems.

And then it all crashed and burned.

My conservative spots must have been showing.

By this time, even though I had been granted tenure by my principal, my conservative principles had run afoul of his liberal agenda. It was around this point in time when he dedicated himself to running me out of the teaching profession. Every day I had to anticipate what attack might be coming and try to outwit this man, who had all the power in this domain. One thing you have to give liberals credit for if nothing else—they are dogged and relentless. And this was long before Trump Derangement Syndrome. In addition, I had to do the work necessary to educate my students.

Now I have a sense of what Donald Trump must go through each day as he fights the Democratic mission of impeachment in search of a crime, and has to fight political opponents as well as the media and still do the work of trying to run the country. I will say that it takes an individual with an enormous amount of energy to withstand this kind of daily assault. Chuck Schumer had it right when he declared "Let me tell you: You take on the intelligence community—they have six ways from Sunday at getting back at you."

It was inevitable that in a system designed to produce conformity and stifle individual creativity, dominated by liberals, that an out-of-the-box conservative thinker would eventually get in trouble with the puppet masters. Never mind that the kids were thriving, because the one thing that you always have to remember, is that it is not really about the kids. They really don't care about the kids, even though they will tell you that they do.

I got in trouble because I ran contrary to the agenda. I didn't fit in with their narrative. It still amazes me that at one point, they thought that not only was I a good fit for this school, but that I was qualified to be offered tenure. All of a sudden, I didn't fit in their box. How could my teaching skills have deteriorated so quickly, when I should have been getting better? Truth be told, they weren't. I was the same teacher in terms of philosophy that I had always been. They just found out more about my politics and what they learned; they didn't like. In essence, I went through a version of what President Trump has gone through since his election, but this was long before the assault on Trump began. I could see the similarities. The end justifies the means. Liberals don't care about the kids if they can use them to get rid of someone they have targeted, just like Democrats don't care about the welfare of the country, (and folks that means all of us) in their quest to take down this president. And they don't stop at just trying to get rid of you, they want to destroy you.

The machine was about to exact their pound of flesh for my insubordination. The first act of retribution was the cancellation of my afterschool class. I was told that they did not have the money to fund all of the afterschool activities. Somehow, my class, which had proven to be the most successful and popular, was the only one that was axed. After my program was cancelled, I remember coming back to my room from a meeting in another part of the school. There were kids lined up outside my room waiting to get in. I decided to defy the DOE and opened my room up even though I wouldn't be getting paid for my time. We flew under the radar for about a week until security was notified not to let students into my room and that effectively ended the afterschool program.

But the personal battle for the minds of the students was just beginning. I had been served notice. They were out to get me. I had no power and my only element of protection was that I had been granted tenure. The strength of that protection was about to be tested. Being a conservative in a liberal education system is a lot like being the roadrunner in a Wile Coyote cartoon. I know younger readers won't appreciate that comparison, but I know President Trump could identify. It means the liberal establishment keeps devising ways to trap you and get rid of you.

"But it is also true that some career officials…have sought ways to thwart Mr. Trump's aims by slow-walking his orders, keeping information from him, leaking to reporters or enlisting allies in Congress to intervene." (New York Times)

I continued my work with the 'Teaching America's Story' program and the 'Globe Science Initiative.' These were independent programs that collaborated with teachers to make them better educators, by supplying them with information and materials that would improve their classrooms. In the course of my association with these organizations, I was able to secure thousands of dollars of grants, equipment and supplies for this Title I school. I was the only teacher from my school that was an active participant in both these organizations, for the entire length of my tenure at this school.

One of the most treasured prizes of working with these organizations was securing a mobile museum visit to your school. The Museum of Natural History (at great expense to them no doubt) had developed three mobile learning centers. These were huge mobile homes that had been converted into rolling exhibits. One was dedicated to dinosaurs, one to astronomy, (associated with the Hayden Planetarium and the famous astrophysicist Neil DeGrasse Tyson) and one was devoted to the study of marine biology.

These mobile units were sent out every day to schools and businesses to serve as teaching instruments and publicity purposes. To get one of these to visit your school for the day, is a real privilege and a feather in the cap of the host school. They park this huge monster in front of your school and the students see it when they come in and classes get to take a tour through it. It creates a lot of excitement and even kids who hate school are curious to see what's inside. Everyone is on their best behavior that day. It is an event that makes local news.

Some schools have never ever gotten a visit from these vehicles. Some schools considered themselves extremely fortunate to have gotten one visit. I was able to qualify our school for three visits in three years, which is almost an unprecedented series of events. I was never given any recognition for this achievement by the administration of my school. Never even as much as a thank you. My reward for doing the best I could for my students was coming up. My principal had devised what he thought was a sure-fire way to bring about my demise. Just another day in the life of a conservative teacher.

Excerpt from A Special Kind of Stupid: The Persecution of an American Educator

One of the Department of Education policies or practices in New York was to separate disruptive learners. The philosophy behind this diffusion was one of divide and conquer. There are many students in the inner-city school system that come to school only because the state law requires them to attend, until they are 16 years old. However, these students have no interest in school or learning and are there solely to be as disruptive as possible--derailing education for everyone.

For some reason school administrations feel it is more prudent to disperse these problematic students over many classes rather than concentrate them in one or two areas. The theory was that a couple of disruptive students could be more readily managed if they were diluted within a classroom, of say 30 kids, who were more disposed to learning. It was even felt that the majority of learners might provide a positive peer influence for the disruptors to conform. As good as it looked on paper, the opposite happened. In most cases, it only took one or two disruptors to destroy the learning atmosphere for the rest of the students in the classroom.

If you ask any teacher, it only takes one or two disruptive students to render the learning process almost impossible for the other students in the class. I have never understood why the school system feels it is necessary to sacrifice the education of 98% of their students while catering to the 2%. Administration's reluctance to remove these students is dangerous, in that it undermines the teacher's authority and it allows an aggressive situation to fester inside the classroom. The kind of behavior exhibited by these students would not be tolerated in any other area of life--at home their parents would punish them, in the street they would be beaten up or arrested and on the job they would be fired--only in the schools does the system empower them to act with virtual impunity.

In my opinion, it came down to a simple case of math. Let's say you had 10 classes of 35 students each and 10 of the 350 were disruptive students. According to the practice of diffusion, one disruptive student would be assigned to each class. If it didn't work and all 10 students continued their disruptive behavior it could have a potential detrimental impact on 350 students. If you grouped all the disruptive students in one class—it allowed 340 to get their education and let's say by some miracle, the teacher of the 10 disruptive students was able to reach 3; the ratio of successful learning is 343/350. In anyone's logic, this was a much better ratio-- although I can't imagine it would have been very enjoyable for the teacher, who had the one class from hell."

However, in a world of inclusion, no child left behind and non-discrimination, administrations are often reluctant to adopt the logical situation and this was always one reason why the learning process was undermined in an inner city environment.

I was about to be the guinea pig in the next experiment. It was the next step in *my education* for being a non-conformist. My school had never adopted the all-the-bad-eggs-in-one-basket practice, at least no one could recall it being tried. Why don't we give it the acronym ATBEIOB, so we can lend some credibility to something that is just made up on the spot-- like most of the other policies that the DOE comes up with. At least now, you and I can converse like *real* teachers do.

I was actually in agreement with the principle behind ATBEIOB, in that it afforded the highest percentage of students in the school the opportunity to be successful. That's what it was supposed to be all about, right, what was best for the kids and what was best for the school. It was setting yourself up to fail, (of course I was no stranger to that concept) with the knowledge that you would be sacrificing yourself for the good of the majority. Kind of noble, actually, when you look at it in that light but make no mistake, this was only designed to create a situation that would be so intolerable that I would resign. The quickest way to get a teacher with tenure out of the system was to make life so miserable that they walk away. This was the next sure-fire campaign that I would have to weather.

At the beginning of one of the semesters ATBEIOB was launched. The next morning I was staring into the sneering faces of twelve of the most disruptive, incorrigible kids in the school. Many of these kids were one step removed from serving time. It was like the Alcatraz of the prison system, where you send all your worst offenders.

I knew just from looking at them that first morning, that it was going to be bad and, in retrospect, it certainly lived up to all expectations. At the time, I was convinced that the administration had finally won. There was no way that I could survive this. But I was determined go down fighting and take it as far as I could.

It was a *classroom* in name only. It was soon apparent that there would not even be the pretense of any learning taking place. It was for all intents and purposes, a holding cell.

The stress level was incredible, and I have to admit that I came close to cracking, on more than one occasion. I can say that now but at the time I tried to keep up the appearance that I was bearing up just fine. I don't think I was really fooling anyone because this was pure hell on wheels and everyone knew it, but in this war that I was engaged in with administration, I didn't want to give them the satisfaction that their plan was working.

There was one fly in the ointment with this whole scheme. I couldn't teach the whole curriculum to this class and other teachers had to be brought in. I had the class for 4 periods every day and 2 other teachers had them for 2 periods each. Because they didn't want this gang of hoodlums travelling very far down the halls, and wreaking their havoc during class changes, the two other classes they had to attend were adjacent to my classroom, one on either side.

I remember each morning before class began, all the teachers would stand in the hallway in front of their classroom doors. The principal would walk down the hall and greet each teacher before the bell rang, signaling the start of the day. I think he fancied himself to be some version of a military officer and we were lining up for inspection.

In my case, I think that it was more a case of checking on a patient with a terminal disease, to see how he was holding up. Every day, I smiled through gritted teeth but I never missed a day. In fact, I earned some extra bonuses in my pay, for perfect attendance. But I would be lying if I said that I was coming through this unscathed.

It was right around this time that I noticed that my hands were beginning to shake. I had to get my students to do anything that required fine motors skills, for me. The ordeal was beginning to take its toll on others, as well. The two teachers on either side of me, were calling in sick more and more and this was putting a strain on the substitutes as well. Substitutes cost money and this negatively impacted the school budget.

In the end, the other two teachers were unable to cope with the CLH (class from hell) and they both resigned. I was also on the verge of doing the same. When no other teachers could be recruited as full-time replacements for the other two classrooms, the whole experiment was abandoned. I think by that point, half the class had been expelled or taken out in handcuffs anyway.

I recall the day that the project was called off, standing in front of my classroom door as the principal made his rounds. I smiled back and saluted as he passed by, as the two locked doors of the abandoned classrooms on both sides of me spoke volumes. Then I stumbled from exhaustion into my room and closed the door. It wasn't until a full year after I had left New York, that my hands finally stopped trembling.

So, in the end I survived, mostly by default and attrition. Like the teacher unions always tried to drum into our heads, it's not how good a teacher you are, it's how good you are at hanging around.

But like the good leftists they are, they were not about to give up. They had only lost the battle, not the war. They had lost two good teachers in the process, but that was just collateral damage in the pursuit of their objective to get rid of me. It was just (SOP), standard operating procedure.

With some of my classes, after we had covered the curriculum that was required, I would use our extra time to examine things that they wanted to learn about, rather than what was dictated to us by the school. Some of the things we looked at in our class was the Titanic, mysteries about the pyramids and the Kennedy assassination. I learned a lot about them from the examination of these various topics.

The Kennedy assassination is a perfect example. This was a historical event of major significance. Of course, I realized the high school students that engaged in this study were born some 40 years after this event happened. Very few had ever heard of Kennedy, knew who he was or that he had been assassinated. However, every November there is no shortage of documentaries, movies and theories presented on television revisiting the event. If anyone had any curiosity whatsoever, the information is readily available. And this is where we are with the condition of our education in this society. No one bothers to seek anything out on their own. Oh sure, the class was fascinated by the events once it was presented to them but I was still stunned that they were so oblivious to the subject and no one else had felt that it was important enough to introduce it to them. We spent time viewing some of the documents, reading some of the material and discussing some of the theories.

I love when the topic is controversial as the Kennedy assassination because at the end, I ask them to write down what they think happened and give their evidence to support it. They were not going to be graded on this because there would be no right or wrong, but this was critical thinking in all its glory. They were presented with a situation and a set of facts and they were going to have to analyze it, come out with a premise and provide evidence that supported that premise. This was a skill that would serve them well for the rest of their lives and as a teacher, I was excoriated for teaching it in the classroom. It was typical MO (modus operandi) for the DOE.

I have a personal example to relate that illustrates just how powerful the critical thinking experience can be. I was always a big proponent of field trips as opposed to classroom and learning out of a book. I think that anytime you can take a student to see a real object or a real place where history has occurred, you are providing the best possible learning experience. Especially as opposed to relying on a graduate just out of a liberal learning factory that has barely read a textbook on the topic and is programmed to present it at the behest of liberal administrators. If you really care about your child's education and want them to truly become aware and comprehend our history, I would advise that you take them to visit as many actual places as you can.

That is an invaluable experience and one that is likely to remain with them and serve them for a longer period. I recently took a trip around the country and I saw and did so many incredible things that I know I will remember and be able to recount for the rest of my life. It gives you a perspective that you just cannot get out of a book or even watching a film. For examples, one of the places we visited was the last stand battlefield of General George Custer.

Now I have read several books on the subject and studied the accompanying maps, but nothing I had done previously brought it more to life for me than standing on the actual battlefield where that event took place. I was able to view the actual terrain, the geography of the area, the logistics of where the soldiers were as opposed to the Indians, what each saw from their particular perspective, what they might have been thinking. And most important, what caused each proponent to act the way that they did. Finally, I was able to see the actual places where the soldiers fell and their final resting places. I felt like I had walked through a door that allowed me to be an observer to a historical event--something that a book or a movie could never achieve. I was moved in a way that could never happen with a book or a movie.

This is the kind of immersion that inspires real learning and I realized that I wish I could have taken every one of my students on that journey. We would have learned so much together and I am talking about genuine learning that sticks to your mind and it becomes an experience that you carry with you for the rest of your life. That to me is a real educated person. Compare that to all the liberal, leftist, college education system graduates whose knowledge is so shallow they cannot tell you who fought in the Civil War.

For an even more profound effect combine critical thinking with a historical event and a visit to a historical site. This is what an exercise in that kind of analytical thinking might look like.

I remember when John F. Kennedy was killed. It was a cool, overcast Friday in late November and the principal came into my fifth-grade class and said that there was an incident with the President of the United States, and we were going to be dismissed early. He did not actually say JFK was dead although I think that had been reported by then, but I think he felt it was better that we got that news when we got home and were with our families.

That was a time when school did not try to be "the be all and end all" to their students and respected parents' rights and their roles in raising their own children When I got home my mother had the television on and it was all over the news and that is when I learned he was dead. Certainly, at that age I would not have been able to grasp the repercussions and significance of the event, but I felt as if I had lost a friend and I felt like crying.

I was pretty invested in JFK and I remember that I had stayed up late the night of the election just a few years before. Finally, my mother had to send me to bed as there was still no result and I had school the next morning. It was not until I got up to go to school the next morning, that I learned that JFK had won the presidency. He was smart, good looking and had a self-deprecating sense of humor that not only captivated me but the whole country.

Over the next few years, he dominated the news (I especially remember the tense days of the Cuban missile crisis) and I thought he was such a great president. And now he was dead. My mother reassured me that someone else would take over and they would be competent enough to run the country and we would all be fine. I guess that was enough assurance to keep me from crying and I went out to play with my friends. Nevertheless, I could not get rid of the feeling of emptiness that we had lost something, our perception that the world was a safe place, our innocence, something I could not put my finger on or articulate at the time. Something I just felt.

Two days later, on a Sunday morning after a somber weekend of watching the nation get ready to bury their president, I saw Jack Ruby kill Lee Harvey Oswald live on television—as it was actually happening in the moment. I was stunned and over the next few years it seemed as if the country had devolved into chaos with Martin Luther King, Robert Kennedy, Vietnam and its protests. We had lost our innocence.

But the JFK assassination always haunted me. I watched the Zapruder film hundreds of times, and other documentaries and books that came out on the subject. I was fascinated with the controversies and the theories and all the conflicting evidence. I guess I always harbored doubts that it was a single shooter but there did not seem to be any concrete evidence for multiple shooters either--although there seemed to be substantial circumstantial evidence.

Over the years, then the decades that followed there was a restlessness there in my mind, that festers like a toothache until you finally go to the dentist and have it taken care of once and for all.

That is what ultimately happened and to me it indicates the power of visiting the actual site of an event. Recently I went to Dallas and there it all was-- just like I had seen it on television and in pictures. Dealey Plaza, the Texas Schoolbook Depository, the grassy knoll, all relatively unchanged from the images I had seen. The first thing that struck me was how compact Dealey Plaza was. I imagined a much larger area but in reality it is quite a tight quartered area, surrounding the street like a small amphitheater surrounding a stage.

There were white "X"s on the street to designate where the motorcade was at the time of each of the three shots, that were fired from the fifth floor window of the school book depository. I stared for an indeterminately longer time at the third "X". That was the third shot that ended the life of a president and changed the course of history for millions of people all over the world.

Some fifty years after I had been a witness to some of these events, I was standing on the spot where it actually happened. I cannot tell you how powerful a moment that was for me--it was like I went back in time and all the emotions and thoughts that I had accumulated over the years washed over me like a wave. I could not hold my emotions back. I cried the tears that I never did when I was a kid because I now had the full weight of the gravity of what occurred here, behind me. But that was only the first of several powerful moments I had that day.

The schoolbook depository is now a museum that has many exhibits and artifacts of the time. As I toured its floors, I was spell bound, until I came to the exhibit on the sixth floor. At the window where Lee Harvey Oswald allegedly fired the three shots in forty seconds, the scene had been set like it was back on that fateful day. There are boxes stacked around the window to conceal the shooter and boxes arranged in front of the window where the gunman could spread out and rest his shoulder to take his shots. It was a recreation of Lee Harvey Oswald's sniper nest.

I could picture him lying there, waiting nervously, looking, waiting as Kennedy's car came up and then turned onto Elm Street and started driving away. The crowd cheering and supposedly him the only one knowing what was about to happen or if it even would. And if it did the chaos that would ensue. The tension of those moments must have been almost unbelievable and yet he would have had to get it under control and stay cool enough to be able to accomplish his task.

As I stood there, I felt chills run up and down my spine. The ramifications of what the man who was right here at that moment-- went back fifty years across a thousand miles, all the way back to a little kid in a fifth-grade classroom and later would stay with him the rest of his life. It was a seminal moment for me, one that I never expected, as it just kind of crept over me, but one that was indelible as I looked out that window and saw the same view that the assassin had that day.

It was if I was looking through the eyes of Lee Harvey Oswald seconds before he was about to pull the trigger and change the world. It was the second profound and powerful moment I had that day but there was one more to come. I exited the museum and went back down to the street, I wandered over to some cement structures on the side of the road. One was marked as the spot where Abraham Zapruder stood as he recorded one of the most significant films ever recorded.

Then I went over to the grassy knoll area. The fence area looked almost exactly as it appeared in 1963. Someone had placed an "X" on one of the fence boards. I knew what this "X" was intended to designate. This was not part of the government narrative. This was supposed to be the spot where it was claimed that a second shooter stood. It was this shooter who was to have fired the fatal third shot at JFK.

I peered over the fence.

In clear sight of this shooter's view loomed the "X" in the street. The place where the third shot struck JFK and ended his life. It was right there in front of me. The logistics of it all was right there. It took a few seconds and then wham--it hit me. One of the few epiphanies of my life but it was undeniable. I began to feel a strange calm come over me, a sense of release, a sense of peace, a sense of closure.

I played it out in my mind all the way back to my hotel and it made sense. It felt right, like putting the last pieces of a jigsaw puzzle together. It felt right, it felt complete. I muttered under my breath to myself, I think I finally figured out what happened here. At least to my way of thinking. I think I can finally put this to rest. I know this is going to sound funny because the assassination of JFK never prayed on my mind--to the point where it kept me awake at night but that night, I had one of the deepest most restful night's sleep of my life. Maybe it had always resided in my subconsciousness.

Here is what I figured out from my visit that day. I just want to say that this is only my theory and it may not work for anyone else, but I am thoroughly convinced that this is how it went down. I believe that there was a shooter in the window of the fifth floor of the schoolbook depository. However, I am not sure it was even Oswald. Oswald's famous statement "I'm just a patsy" lends some credence to that line of thinking. And that he was killed in order to silence him is also highly conceivable.

When I was in the sniper's den on the sixth floor and I looked at the sightline through the eyes of the sniper I asked myself one question, "Why did he wait?" First, let me qualify I am not an expert shooter. I have had a little gun training, I have been a hunter, and I have played in some recreational war games but when I asked this question-- it was just from an average person's common-sense point of view.

Let me explain. The sixth-floor window had excellent views of two streets, Houston Street and Elm Street. On that day Kennedy's car came up Houston toward the Texas book depository at an estimated 20-25 miles per hour after it turned right off Main, then it slowed dramatically to 10 miles per hour or less right in front of the schoolbook depository. As it made a left onto Elm Street slowly picking up speed, it moved away from the sniper.

It has always been true even in my limited experience that a target that is moving towards you is infinitely easier to hit than a target that is moving away--but the sniper did not take that opportunity to shoot. Not only was Kennedy's car moving toward the sniper but it practical stopped and posed-- like it was suspended in slow motion and pausing for a picture at the closest possible proximity to the shooter. If I did not know better, I would say that someone was presenting the president in the best target position possible, almost like when you have a deer in your sights, and it turns sideways giving the hunter the ideal shot. The sniper had that ideal situation with the president's car in precisely a state of suspended animation at the base of the schoolbook depository building and still the sniper did not shoot.

He waited.

Now the car (Kennedy) was moving away and picking up speed-- both adverse conditions to a successful strike. Finally, with the Kennedy car moving away from the sniper it is believed he fired his first shot, which missed everything and struck the road pavement. A second shot struck Kennedy and Governor Connelly via (the magic bullet) and the third shot was the furthest away from the schoolbook depository and the fatal shot to President Kennedy. Back to my question of why a shooter would wait for an option that had the least chance of success, before he opened fire.

If it was a lone shooter as the official record wants the public to believe he would have considered option one, with the target moving towards him as a more viable option, option two with the President almost stationary and in closest proximity as the ultimate option, but the sniper waited for the third option which guaranteed the least possible successful outcome.

The key lies in the fact the shooter was not alone and he knew it. That explains why he bypassed his first two options, because he was waiting for the President's car to get in the optimum position for multiple shooters to come into play. This makes sense and so to my mind I was convinced there was more than one shooter and at least two. That was confirmed in my mind when I peered over the fence at the grassy knoll.

That was the kill shot without a doubt. A target moving slowly in your direction right in the wheelhouse of your cross hairs. I knew then that it was a conspiracy to kill the President--no matter what I had been told to the contrary over the past fifty years. It was my moment of epiphany and it would never have occurred if I had not taken the time and effort to visit the site.

My final assessment of this matter that Kennedy was set up to enter this theatre (the intimate and enclosed area of the Dealey Plaza) which was to provide a kind of triangulation deathtrap. It was a killing zone which was designed to allow the President to enter but in which he would never be allowed to come out alive. I am convinced it was an organized, premeditated, assassination conspiracy. Who was responsible? I have my theories on that as well in a later section of this book.

The point of this is to illustrate that when a person is presented with a piece of information, they need to be able to assess it for themselves. They need to examine the sources and take into account possible motives. It would benefit them to do some independent investigation or research some other accounts and gather as much pertinent evidence as possible. A logical person would then take the evidence and analyze it and then make an informed decision. This is what critical thinking looks like and it allows you to synthesize information. It leads to intelligent, responsible and independent decisions.

What I'm about to say next is going to shock some people. Not only does the left wing of this country not care about the quality of education, even though they pretend to, they would prefer uneducated students. That is exactly what they want by *design*. And the education system is just a microcosm for what the left wants to do to the rest of society. It's their (MO) modus operandi.

It is no wonder that analysis and synthesis is not being taught in our schools because this is the last thing that the left wants. The last thing they want is to turn out independent, critical thinkers because that runs completely contrary to a low information voter. A person who can think for themselves is not likely to take a sound bite like "Trump is bad" and accept it on its face value. A critical thinker might want to investigate that statement and come to their own conclusion. And the left does not want to leave that conclusion to chance.

They do not want there to be any doubt that their constituents will deviate in any way from their dictates and not follow the party line. They want sheep to accept whatever they say as if it were the truth and go to the ballot box and pull the lever for whoever the left designates as their candidate every four years.

Does this sound like a vibrant democracy in action? It sounds more like a robotic Manchurian Candidate programmed to do the bidding of an elitist few, who in order to perpetuate its power will sacrifice whole generations of our youth.

It took me awhile, but I realized that liberals and the left who are running our school do not want critical thinkers coming out of their system. They want malleable sheep. Moreover, a process is needed to accomplish this. Therefore, they try to erase the history of the country and the ideals and principles that it was founded on. Then they replace these events with their own version, one that serves their agenda and espouses their beliefs and principles. Religion and families are bad so do not listen to them and the state will provide you with everything you need from cradle to grave.

The left has been very good at recognizing that the youth of this country was its future and they have been very successful in indoctrinating with its agenda, and the reward for all this hard work by the left is the kind of society we have now. Where our younger generation has a meltdown if they are faced with any type of adversity and political correctness is the rule and if you ask a young person who won the Civil War, all you get is crickets.

I have always said that liberals are specialists at creating captive audiences. That's the only way that most of the teachers in the school system have any students in their classroom, because the law requires them to be there. God forbid, that the DOE trained teachers to be interesting and engaging enough, that a student might want to attend their class of their own volition. I was in a seminar once, where the lecturer was telling a group of teachers how to be more engaging-- and she delivered her instruction in the most monotone, uninspiring, disconnected presentation I have ever witnessed. Talk about teaching by example.

The education system is just a microcosm of what liberals will do when they get control of our lives. They want sheep who are dependent on them for everything and will do what they tell them to do without question.

But that is exactly the kind of product the left wants coming out of their liberal processing plants. When the process was just starting to evolve we used to call it the "dumbing down of America," now we call it a "special kind of stupid" but it goes beyond that. Liberals want to erase the values that this country was founded on, and replace them with their own brand of ideals.

This was always the grand design.

The Democrats would infiltrate the education system and foster in our youth this special kind of stupid (SKOS). Then along with the complicit media the Democratic party could promote their agenda, and nobody would question it, and they would parlay that special brand of stupidity into a perpetuity of power. If a liberal says something they want their constituents to take it on face value and not question it. If a liberal says it, it must be true. The ultimate goal is for the left to be able to tell their constituents who to vote for and then they will always have power. But the cost is our freedom.

The Hunter and Joe Biden affair is a perfect example of how this special kind of stupid works. Hunter Biden was given lucrative deals to be on the boards of foreign energy companies not long after his father who was vice president at the time was put in charge of overseeing foreign affairs in the same countries that hired Hunter Biden.

The problem with this scenario is that Hunter Biden just happens to have no experience whatsoever, in energy. But what he does have is access to the vice presidency of the United States. So, the Democrat vice president says there was nothing going on here. And remarkably everyone on the left takes those words at their face value. The complicit media who take their marching orders from the Democratic party (something that the election of Donald Trump has exposed completely) do not look into the affair to find the truth. Forasmuch as a legitimate news organization would be charged to do, they neglect the truth but print the propaganda that the Democrat has proclaimed. If everything was on the up and up as Joe Biden claimed, then why did his son resign his position from the board shortly after the whole scam was exposed? No one on the left has ever dared to ask that question.

That is the problem when most of the press is in the leftist tank, a Democrat is not used to responding to a real question because all they get are softballs. It is no wonder that Joe Biden is able to go on with his endless stories about how he was a lifeguard in his younger days, and he was able to save civilization from the likes of "Cornpop" and his gang. It is exactly this kind of treatment by the press that enables a Joe Biden to be a politician for what seems like hundreds of years and has never been on the right side of any issue. But to hear Biden tell it, he authored this legislation and that legislation and next thing he will have us believing that he wrote the Constitution (the left-wing press might fall for it because he appears to be old enough to have been there). Another former vice-president, Al Gore had us believing that he invented the internet. What is it about these vice presidents that they feel they have to make themselves seem more important than merely a second banana? They become LITOM(legends in their own minds.)

Case in point: Biden was asked a question by a reporter from a conservative entity for once, about his role in eliminating terrorist leaders. "Oh yeah, we did that with Osama Bin Laden." Apparently the reporter had a better memory than Biden and was not going to let Biden off the hook so easily. He retorted "Wasn't it true that you advised Obama against taking that action?" Biden responded "No."

However, there is a video from that period of time where Biden states in his own words that he was against the assassination of Bin Laden. Biden in a pathetic attempt to curry the African-American vote always states that he had Barack Obama's back for eight years and that is why black people should vote for him. However, what is more telling about Biden in the eyes of black people is that Obama declines to endorse Biden. So then Biden makes the claim that he was in South Africa fighting Apartheid and was arrested with Nelson Mandela. That should get the African-American vote but the problem is there is no record of Biden's LIHOM claim. If it were left to Biden's memory he would somehow magically appear at the center of every important world changing event when the sad reality is that for someone who has been in politics for half a century, he has almost nothing to show for it. His impact on the world stage is almost non-existent. Revisionist history is such a wonderful tool if you are a Democrat and your goal is to be a legend in your own mind.

How far this country has fallen.

I suppose that I could cite plenty of statistics that show how American is on the high end of spending money on education and how our students are on the lower end of the learning spectrum. We mentioned the Asian study earlier, but statistics are not needed to tell parents today what they already know. They are getting very little bang for their buck. The American education system is an abject failure and I can tell you is not an accident.

It is by design.

After 15 years of working in a profession that I loved, but in a system that I loathed, my advice is to never send your child to a public school. Send them to a charter school, home school them, encourage them to read on their own, travel with them whenever you can, anything, but don't send them to a public school.

Parents are increasingly taking responsibility for the education of their children and the trend to homeschooling is growing.

"By 2010 it was well over 3% and growing ever faster. Parents chose home schooling from the reasons that differ little from those that led another 4% of Americans to pay for private schooling and 7 percent to pay for religious (mostly Catholic) schooling. These are the same reasons why parents of public school children clamor for charter schools. In short, one out of seven sets of parents has already abandoned the public schools and many more wish they could…. Small rural public schools are a special case because parents can influence the content and standards of education. They typically have the lowest per pupil expenditures…and produce America's highest SAT scores." (The Ruling Class)

The internet has made homeschooling more user friendly. "The result is that SAT scores for home schoolers hover around the eightieth percentile. How did those dumb violent racists achieve results like that?" (The Ruling Class)

Consider this, Liberals are "advocating a direct relationship between the government and children," effectively abolishing the presumption of parental authority. Hence, whereas within living memory school nurses could not administer an aspirin to a child without the parents' consent, the people who run America's schools nowadays administer pregnancy tests and ship girls off to abortion clinics without the parent's knowledge." (The Ruling Class) There was an incident on the news recently where a first-grade class was discussing Santa Claus. Of course, it was not unexpected that at such an early age many of these students still believed in Santa Claus. Apparently, this first-grade teacher felt it was her place to set the record straight when she proclaimed, "Your parents are liars." This should send chills down the spine of every parent who has a child in the school system.

So, mission accomplished. The college graduates of today are dumb as a rock, brainwashed of American principles, taught to hate our country and programmed to accept the marching orders from the left without question. The result of all their control is that the United States spends more money per student than any other country and we rank 37th in the world in achievement. Now they want to take over the other segments of our society. Phase I is complete. The table is set. Phase II is to find a complicit accomplice.

In the end what did we learn from our foray into the workings of the education system?

Someone who can think is a danger to themselves.

Someone who can question and think is a danger to the state.

"We don't need no mind control"

"Teacher leave those kids alone"

THE STATE OF THE MEDIA
IN AMERICA

"If you once forfeit the confidence of your fellow citizens, you can never regain their respect and esteem. It is true that you may fool all of the people some of the time; you can even fool some of the people all of the time; but you can't fool all of the people all of the time." (Abraham Lincoln)

"We'll know our disinformation program is complete when everything the American public believes is false. (William Casey, former CIA director)

There was no Nazi-like coercion of the media in this country to adopt a one-sided propaganda agenda. The news media did that all on their own. They were always left leaning, but when they abdicated the search for truth they became dangerous. They were the coveted accomplice that was needed to work hand in hand with a dumbed down and compliantly suggestible electorate. It was a match made in liberal leftist heaven.

You don't have to look any further than your cable newscast for confirmation of this devil's pact. On any particular day, there will be a "catchword of the day" or phrase that is faithfully repeated by every leftist commentator like a mantra. It is almost as if someone from the top somewhere is issuing the word of the day. Moreover, the way you can identify it is because it is usually a little bit outside the general usage lexicon of the average person.

A perfect example was the phrase "solemn occasion" whenever the topic of impeachment is discussed. Therefore, when you keep hearing this 'outside the norm phrase', over and over again on different channels by different news people and different guests, it is easy to conclude that they have been given their marching orders, so that they will all be in a united lockstep. What are the chances that they would all be on the same page without directed coordination? The only question about this coordination is whether the news media is dictating to the Democrat Party or it is the other way around.

Mark Levin in his book "The Unfreedom of the Press" was referring to a free and fair press when he stated "That it is essential to the operation of the economy and to the government of the Republic."

What's implied in these quotes is that our Constitution was such a rare soup that it may have only occurred through the coming together of a unique blend of ingredients; the right circumstances and intellect. And the only way to preserve the Constitution and the Republic is through an *educated* and *informed* citizenry. The consequences of undermining the precepts of 'educated and informed' has direct and detrimental implications on our Constitution and Republic. In the previous section, we have seen how the education system has done its part to sabotage an "educated citizenry". It is the job of a free and responsible press to produce an 'informed citizenry'.

That responsibility was once so sacred that there was a time when the press was regarded as the fourth estate.

Our fourth estate has become a fifth column, meaning they have become an opposing force within the walls of the Republic colluding with the enemy outside, to bring about the downfall of democracy.

Consider the incestuous relationship between the media and the Democrat party. Mark Levin in his book "The Unfreedom of the Press" has entire lists of people who have crossed over for one entity to the other. They are virtually interchangeable.

In Clint Eastwood's movie "Richard Jewell" the main character is railroaded by a reporter who allegedly sleeps with a law enforcement official to get information. I think that is exactly what they had in mind when the coined the phrase "in bed" with. Education, the Democrat Party, and the news media are all in bed with each other. It's also what the Germans meant by 'synchronization'.

Consider this. Most of the news media outlets were touting for years that the Trump campaign had colluded with Russian assets to influence the 2016 election. This was the drum beat of the mainstream media for two and a half years. When the Mueller report came out and declared that there was no collusion and that it was likely a false assertion from the beginning (incidentally at a cost of 40 million dollars, over 2 years and at the risk of dividing the country even further), the nature of the investigation began to shift to the suspicious origins of the false accusations. As a result, the report from Inspector General Horowitz implicated certain players, inside the CIA and FBI. Two of those players Andrew McCabe and James Clapper who are objects of an ongoing criminal investigation were hired by CNN as commentators--to give an analysis of the investigation on themselves. Folks, bias is one thing but how can the hiring of those two individuals to report on the news, be viewed as anything but a complete and compromised conflict of interest. As an average citizen, is that the source that you would want to be getting your information from? With sources that have such a vested self interest in the outcome, how could anything they say not be tainted or to use the common phrase of the times "fake news."

Even more blatantly, these same news outlets who were also purporting for years, that any misconduct over the origins of what turned out to be a "hoax", was just a conspiracy theory and that there was no abuse of the FISA application process--were conspicuously absent when the IG's report was released and it revealed that there *was* extensive abuse.

That report was ground-breaking news that shed profound revelations on the conduct of two of our most trusted institutions and these outlets were nowhere in sight. Why? Because the evidence refuted the false narrative "bubble" that they had been reporting to their constituents for years. In fact, for CNN viewers it must have been really cutting edge. It would likely have been one of the first times they would have heard of such a dossier. The absence of reporting the truth is disingenuous and no less a sabotage of the truth--than a lie. The "bubble" is everything to the leftist media. The bubble is an alternate ecosystem created out of words taken out of context, one side of the story reporting, strategic omissions of the truth, outright lies, and untruthful fabrications (or "fake news") to feed a preordained narrative that has no relevance to reality. The bubble is the antithesis of reality and the truth.

Think about what happens when you literally create a bubble. It is manufactured from a mixture of soap ingredients and is manipulated across an opening to construct a bubble and disseminated through the air. It is like a separate cell that has its interior insulated from the exterior environment. It floats along merrily, oblivious to what is around it, until it bumps into a sharp object and bursts. That object is reality.

There is a weathercast that I watch that displays a meter on their screen indicating the weatherman's confidence in the accuracy of that particular forecast. Imagine if the liberal cable news stations were to employ such a meter, indicating the level of truth they were reporting. I'm willing to bet that none of them would be able to move their needle even into the "truthful once in a while" territory and it would be mostly mired in the "complete bullshit all the time" zone.

If you were to watch these mainstream media outlets exclusively for any length of time you would have no idea of what is really happening. I have friends in other countries who have limited access to American news sources except perhaps to a CNN and they have such a shaped and distorted viewpoint of the American landscape, that I can't even recognize it as the same country that I live in. CNN is doing such a great job of attracting viewers that they pay 58 airports in cities across the country, over 6 million dollars yearly to have the televisions at the passenger gates tuned in to CNN. I always maintained that liberals are specialists at engaging captive audiences.

James Comey, another object of investigation in the IG Horowitz report, was interviewed by Chris Wallace of Fox News on 12/15/19. Previously he had maintained no evidence of wrong-doing, although the IG report found evidence to the contrary. He was asked direct questions of the recently revealed facts in the report. It was apparently the first time that he had to face these kinds of questions. These were not the kind of questions that would be asked in the "bubble" over at the mainstream media outlets. There is nothing more remarkable than watching someone who lives in that "bubble" reacting to the bursting of that "bubble" by reality. The whole squirming interview was a clinic in weasel-ization, deflection, denial and Comey doublespeak. Maybe the viewers cultivated by the current education system and the leftist mainstream media would fall for this delusional attempt at maintaining his innocence, hook, line and sinker. But the *average* American sees right through it.

Lincoln quote: " You can only fool *some* of the people all of the time."

The other "some" of the people obviously went to school before the liberals took over the system and don't get their information from "fake news" outlets.

At the conclusion of the interview, Comey was still in the "bubble of delusion" that he is not going to jail because it was "all made up." According to the evidence of FISA abuse in the Horwitz IG report, if anyone is an expert on fabricating false facts, it is Jim Comey. That's one bubble that Jim Comey is praying doesn't burst.

The election of Donald Trump in 2016 was the celebration of another "bubble burst". Through the lens of the mainstream media, Donald Trump was given about as much chance of winning the 2016 election as a piece of cheddar has of surviving a wine and cheese tasting, for a convention of white mice. We would find out later that those were generous odds.

Conservatives always knew that liberals and the media were arrayed against Trump but then we would learn that so too was the FBI, and certain internal elements of the government (what some refer to as the "deep state") so much so that they attempted to spy on his campaign. It was a miracle that Trump was even competitive, never mind that somehow, he pulled off a victory. That was the "bubble" that the mainstream media created for themselves and their viewers. The people asking the disingenuous questions on these channels are hard to distinguish from the people who are giving the disingenuous answers. It's like a circular lying squad. The polls were misreported and manipulated to create an illusion of a sure thing for Hillary Clinton, and to suppress the vote on the Republican side.

I went to a Trump campaign rally in January of 2016, because I wanted to check things out for myself. This was even before any of the Republican Party debates. There were a lot of stories out there about him and many in the media were mocking the credibility of his campaign. The rally was being held at night at a high school auditorium. We got there about an hour before the advertised start time, figuring that would allow us plenty of time to get in.

Not only that but it was a brutally frigid night and we didn't want to have to stand outside for too long. We were stunned when we got there. The line to get in the venue was four deep and snaked around the school. The people who were already in line, had stood in that kind of cold for hours. Our biggest concern was that we would wait in line and brave the cold and be turned away at the door because the venue was full. We decided to take a chance and luckily, we were among the last people to get admitted. It was a different kind of experience. I sensed that there was a real connection between this candidate and the crowd, something that I had rarely seen before.

It was then, almost a year before the election, that I was convinced that this man would win the Republican nomination and had a real shot at winning the presidency. Of course, every time I mentioned it to other people, I was only met with derision.

The local media played down the attendance of that rally and tried to dismiss it by explaining that turnout at a rally never translates to numbers at the poll. There was some truth to that. Four years before, I had attended a Romney rally just before the election, at one of the largest venues in New Hampshire. The numbers of people who showed up and the energy level they exuded, had convinced me that he was staging a late surge that could result in a national victory. How wrong I was. Romney could not even carry New Hampshire.

Having suffered that disappointment I had to ask myself how would the Trump rally I attended, be any different of an indicator this time. I concluded that there were two differences. Trump seemed to have a rarely seen connection with the audience, because of his style and his message. The second thing was that nobody endures that kind of brutal cold for hours and then doesn't take the time to go and vote. I was convinced that these people would break down doors to get into a voting booth on election day.

And that's exactly what happened. The Clinton campaign was so assured of victory that they had rented the cavernous Javits Center for their victory celebration. The lamestream media was confidently portraying it as a foregone conclusion. As a conservative, I have to admit it was one of the greatest election nights ever. Every time Trump won a state, a corresponding amount of air escaped from the bubble, and the more perplexed the looks on the faces of the news anchors got, and a little less confident were the smiles of the Clinton supporters.

By the end of the night, the news anchors were in stunned denial and Clinton supporters were in tears and Clinton herself was in complete breakdown mode. She was so overwhelmed that it took her until the next day to deliver her concession speech. That's what it looks like when you live in a bubble and it bumps into reality and bursts. Liberals have never been able to accept the fact that they lost the 2016 election and that is one of the reasons that there is such a schism in the country today--over 3 years later.

"Journalism's first obligation is to the truth.

Its first loyalty is to citizens.

Its essence is a discipline of verification.

Its practitioners must maintain an independence from those they cover." Unfreedom of the Press

Of course, every one of these tenets has been violated by the mainstream media. In doing so they have done considerable damage to the country, the constitution and our liberty. They have destroyed their credibility for the foreseeable future. They have rendered our country indistinguishable from the statist propaganda model of Nazi Germany.

"In terms of quality, the information provided must be provided in such a form, and with so scrupulous a regard for the wholeness of the truth and the fairness of its presentation, that the American people may make for themselves, by the exercise of reason and of conscience, the fundamental decisions necessary to the direction of their government and of their lives."

From Mark Levin's Unfreedom of the Press:

> Not only has our press abdicated its mandate to render the truth to the American people, but the education system has rendered the liberal American electorate incapable of distinguishing the truth or making a critical decision.

One final thought before we close out this section.

Professor Lawrence Tribe on Chris Matthews show on November 14, 2019 quoted this "anybody who votes for Trump is a disgusting human being." Matthews responded, "that was a great moral judgement and I wish I was in your classroom."

That's everything you need to know. The news media in bed with the Democrats and education. The royal triumvirate of liberal power all in one declaration. Now that's "synchronization" personified. *Something* the Nazi Party would have been proud of. Throw in a little deep state and you've got the frosting on the cake. There's a lot to unpack here.

I've had many jobs in my lifetime, starting at about age 12 from caddying at a golf course, picking cherries, to delivering newspapers, to construction, to working in a steel mill, to salesman, an electronic technician and most recently educator. In my last profession I earned two masters and a doctorate degree. I have met all kinds of people and in all kinds of lines of work and in a recent trip across the country where I met people from all walks of life and of different political persuasions. I have friends from both sides of the political spectrum that I met in different phases of my life, that I still stay in touch with, that go all the way back to my childhood. Many of these people are smart, funny, kind, caring, successful, poor, wealthy, independent, democrat, and republican. I grew up as a conservative and have been conservative all my life, yet many of my friends, outside of a small circle of friends and family, consider me to be apolitical because engaging in politics is a quick way to end a friendship or lose a job. As many conservatives know, you have to learn to separate politics from your paycheck. If only that were true of liberals on the other side of the aisle. It is one thing to espouse your political beliefs and affiliations on your own time but to have it impact your job performance is a whole different matter.

In the recent IG Horwitz report political bias was the central theme. Did FBI agents who are supposed to be representatives of neutral agencies engage in activities motivated only by their political persuasions? We saw the political bias in the emails between FBI agents Peter Strzok and Lisa Page but did that carry over into the workplace and impact policy? I was a conservative in the education system and there is no question that my bias would have leaked out inadvertently in the everyday performance of my duties. But I never intentionally or consciously taught my bias.

What I mean by that was that my lessons never included the content that reflected a conservative agenda. Unlike the liberals who have injected their agenda of pro-Democratic, anti-Christianity, bisexualism, transgenderism, globalism, socialism and environmentalism into the curriculum. That is unabashed state sanctioned indoctrination.

The only thing I ever tried to teach my students was personal responsibility and to think critically and for that I was persecuted. I wonder if Professor Lawrence Tribe can make the same claim in his classroom--the one that Chris Mathews so desperately wants to attend.

The takeaway from all of this; "Ye shall know the truth and the truth shall make you free" (John 8:32).

If truth is not the objective of the media, then they have become the enemy of the people.

THE STATE OF SOCIETY IN AMERICA.

"Do y'all remember, before the internet, that people
thought the cause of stupidity was the lack of access to
information? Yeah. It wasn't that." (Facebook meme from
Crazy World)

"Liberalism is a mental disorder." (Michael Savage)

The education system was always the template. It was always the
microcosm for what the left wing wanted to do to the rest of the
country. They enlisted a complicit and corrupted news media in an
endless assault of mind control on our young unsuspecting citizenry
and the result is the creation of yet another bubble.

Today's society is afflicted by the "snowflake bubble". The
"snowflake bubble" is filled with air from the over-inflated self-
esteem. It too, as we saw with other bubbles, has no foundation in
reality. In this case, it has no relevance to earned achievement. It
stems from the liberal concept that everyone deserves a trophy. It is
a protective cocoon created from an illusion of how wonderful they
think life is until they are confronted with adversity and then they
melt, hence the term 'snowflake'.

Liberals feel they can say anything to attack conservatives but if
they are criticized in the slightest, they cannot handle it. In real life,
if you want to dish it out, you better learn to take it. Someone forgot

to tell the liberals about that part. They expect it to be only one way--their way. This is why they hate Trump--he fights back and they can't cope with it. This concept was central to my previous book even though it was written in the context of a study on school shooters.

Excerpt from SSTOP
The Eggshell Analogy NEST-nurtured eggshell theory

To achieve its intent this work will follow a framework, of what I term NEST, the nurtured eggshell theory. This is a simple process that encompasses three premises. The first premise is that our society and culture is turning out over-protected, over-sensitive personalities (translated--pristine, unblemished eggs delivered from the nest) whose fragility is as delicate as an eggshell. The second premise is that they are ill-equipped to deal with stress (in particular the stressor of bullying in the school setting) and other pressures of life and each one has the potential to crack. The shell (which is the thin veneer represented by their individual coping skills) is their only protection against these stressors. Some will withstand the pressure, some won't. Think of it like a carton of eggs, with each egg being squeezed in turn. The third premise is that knowing a little information about the makeup of each egg before it is squeezed, will help us to determine which eggs are LIKELY to crack. And to achieve that end, we will use the application of a personality determinant known as the Myers-Briggs Type Indicator. Our modern society has incubated more eggs (potential candidates for cracking) than ever before. The question before us is, can we diagnose which ones are most likely to crack before we end up with a pile of broken eggshells?

The Absence of Adversity

There's no doubt that the world of today in which our children are growing up in is a vastly different place than the one that we, as their parents, experienced. That doesn't necessarily mean it is a better place, although we certainly hoped that it would be. Every parent wants their child to have it better than they themselves did. It is a noble premise indeed, but therein lies the problem. The pendulum may have swung too far. I came from a generation where we didn't have a lot of frills. All we needed was a ball and a stick and a little space and we could find a way to entertain ourselves for hours on end. We didn't need to be organized into a league with a lot of adult supervision. Our parents were the ones who had cut us loose for the day and we were quite capable of devising our own rules of the game. It wasn't perfect but we settled our own differences and parents rarely intervened. We learned to negotiate, compromise, argue, bully sometimes and even fight, to advance our viewpoint but it was all part of the education of personal interaction. Games were for fun but they were also for competition. People played to win, to develop skills and to get better. One way to gain the respect of your peers was to be good at something. Competition fostered that esteem, built character and helped us to stay in good physical condition.

Television was in its infancy at the time. Most households had one black and white, if they were lucky and programming was limited. I can remember many mornings staring at a test pattern, waiting for the network to run its Saturday morning slate of cartoons. Parents in that day would never have stood for allowing their kids to sit in front of a television all day. We were kicked outside, especially if it was a nice day. Many of us had jobs at an early age in life that would have precluded extended time in front of the set. And there were no remote controls. When your parents came home from work they took control of the program selection. If you wanted to watch, you sat in the living room with them, kept quiet and watched what they watched. They paid for the set, so it was ludicrous to think that they were going to work all day and let their kids dictate what to watch. If you didn't like what they were watching. Tough. If you expressed your objections too loudly, you'd better watch out because you might get a cuff on the side of the head. This was an era where parental authority was rarely challenged and corporal punishment was accepted. If you didn't want to be their remote control system, you were better off going outside and playing. Television had its place and it was not allowed to dominate your life.

Speaking of employment, I remember always working as a kid, as did most of my friends. Aside from the household chores of dish washing, taking out the garbage, cutting grass, and shoveling snow, for which you may or may not have been compensated, you might do similar services for other households in the neighborhood. Other jobs I held before I turned 16, included newspaper delivery, washing cars, house painting, working on a farm, picking fruit, pin setting at a bowling alley, babysitting and golf caddy. Since then, I have been a construction worker, tobacco picker, steel worker, factory and warehouse worker, salesman, fast food worker, truck driver, electronic technician and educator. Having a job develops responsibility, work ethic and I always found that working at a job I didn't particularly like inspired me to find something better and acquire the skills necessary to get into that position. Having a job- built character.

Compare that to today when many of our children have never held a job. Some attribute that to the poor economic situation in recent years and that may be true to an extent. But the fact is that many of our youth feel that these menial jobs are beneath them. I had one employer tell me recently that" I have openings—these young workers just don't want to get their hands dirty."

As a result they have not developed any job skills. They don't know how to interview for a position, or interact appropriately with their boss and their co-workers, if they are hired. They are unwilling to work their way up the ladder. They don't want to deal with any adversity and as long as their parents are willing to provide them with all the comforts of home (food, shelter, a computer and a television) there is no incentive for them to come out of their reality-insulated cocoons. I don't mean to get political, but this country is having a difficult time controlling illegal immigration. Historically, this is a problem that is diminished during times of high unemployment, but our youth, by their refusal to accept menial jobs and manual labor, has been responsible for providing unprecedented opportunities for that segment of our population. Some want to lay the blame at the feet of business owners but what's an employer to do when they can't find workers from the traditional sources.

In our time, there was no such thing as the internet. And the minute that you went out to play with your friends all your social skills were put to the test. You had to interact with real people and that meant being conversant, communicating and creating your own little niche in life, with an identity and its own strengths and weaknesses. It was a way to get information and to learn about life. Exposure to other people-built character.

Contrast that with the electronic world we live in now. Everything is at the touch of a finger. Most household have a color flat-screen television in every room with hundreds of channels via cable and satellite. Television is eminently available every minute of the day, with its generous offerings of gratuitous sex and violence and our children have had these electronic companions woven into the very fabric of their lives- at the expense of their physical and social development. Hollywood has supplanted the role of parents when it comes to dictating what morals and principles our children should have. Fake reality television shows substitute for real life and everybody wants the spotlight on them Everyone is carrying instant communication devices and cameras and they rarely look up from these devices even in the presence of others I once saw two young people on a first date at a restaurant and neither one looked at each other or spoke--they were so absorbed in their electronic devices. And everyone wants to be noticed and if I can't be for something good, then something bad will do just as well.

The schools of our day were designed for learning. You learned basics, how to read and write add and subtract without electronic assistance. You did it in your head or on paper, you memorized, you learned to spell. The school didn't try to be the be-all-and-end-all of society's shortcomings. They were only one component of society. If you didn't comply with the rules, they could also use corporal punishment to get their point across. Teachers had earned a certain respect in the community and when they reported your misbehavior to your parents, it was a very rare day indeed if your parents chose to side with you. Schools of that day helped you to learn right from wrong and you could be singled out just as readily for something good that you did, as well as for something bad. That also built character.

The schools of today are forced into the roles that society has defaulted on. They are expected to be parents, babysitters, social centers, nutritionist and doctor's offices, where everyone gets credit for trying and there is no need to correct papers with the trauma of red ink. Where vocational schools are almost non-existent, where no child is left behind, where helicopter parents sit in the classroom and everyone goes to college. Incidentally it is being reported that parents are having a more difficult time than ever pushing their children out of the nest and off to college. Many colleges have established parent centers on campuses. Thirty and even twenty years ago this was unheard of. Parents want to hear from their child every day and some post the student's schedule at home, so they know where they are and what they are doing at all times of the day. Many colleges are reporting that they have to impose strict regulations to get these helicopter parents to leave the campus. Even when these drastic rules are imposed, parents have been observed spying on their child's activities with binoculars and telescopes. This is the culture we have created-- where the United States ranks 1st in student self-esteem but 30th in academic achievement. Where a Massachusetts veteran high school teacher and the son of famous author David McCullough was recently castigated for trying to instill some reality into a graduation ceremony by telling a graduating class that they were no more special than all other graduating classes. Where the educational setting has become a more dangerous place than ever before.

The result of all this over protectiveness and coddling is that all the adversity has been removed. You get the trophy for just showing up. Electronic devices have eliminated the need for personal interaction. Without interaction there is no confrontation, no conflict--therefore no need to develop the skills to deal with these situations. We have scrubbed and sanitized the grit of life needed to develop personality, principles, morals and character. We have not prepared this generation for the ups and downs of life or given them the skills needed to cope with adversity. We have not represented the truth and as a result this generation is ill-equipped to handle it. What we have done is to deliver a nicely formed egg, with no cracks or dents onto the doorstep of college campuses and employers and now that fragility will be tested in the pressure cooker of life's storms. Whether our intentions were good or not, we have done this generation a disservice. And the impact will be felt by all of us."

What this is saying is that when many of our fragile children run their "snowflake bubbles" into reality and are burst, our children are unable to cope with that kind of adversity. Sometimes they lash out and take their frustrations on the rest of society-- and some become school shooters.

It was a declaration that was warning us that school shootings were likely to increase. That prediction has come true as school shootings have increased, exponentially. But the impact is felt in all aspects of society.

It manifests itself in the oppressive nature of political correctness and the 'me too' movement. It is evident in "everybody gets a trophy" and elimination of competition, safe zones and spaces and the coddling and protecting of kids from every possible danger. It shows up in the neutralization of sexual identities and same sex marriages and gender-neutral bathrooms. It appears in open borders, socialistic tendencies, and lack of a work ethic. It is apparent in the decline of God in society and the removal of God in schools, the breakdown of families, increased homelessness, lawlessness and mass shootings. Ironically it seems as if we are prohibited from disagreeing with anyone and yet we have never been more divisively in *disagreement,* than anyone can recall.

In addition to the "snowflake bubble", the leftists in conjunction with the perverted media, have created a mentality conducive to their purposes and an atmosphere of hate, also predisposed to their purposes. Foremost that have created a programmed voting bloc. All they had to say was conservatives are bad, bad, bad. Take our word for it. No need to investigate on your own. No need to find facts or rationale on your own and don't even question it. Accept it for its face value. We are telling you so it must be true. Especially since we will repeat it over and over again. *Only* three times a day--morning, noon and night. So, go vote democratic and on the way to the voting booth don't forget to stop in at the school and thank your teachers, for us, for a job well done. But even that wasn't enough to win the 2016 election.

Then the mentality became to not accept the results of an election. Remember when everybody gets a trophy there are no losers. Except in real life there are winners and losers and losing an election has consequences. Sorry to burst your bubble but you don't get to run the country. Thank the media for deluding you.

Enter the mentality of trying to run a coup within the justice department to take down a president,(which I predict will become the biggest political scandal and abuse of power in American history when all the facts come out) overturn the results of an election, and deny 63 million Americans their constitutional right to vote.

Sorry to burst your bubble again, but these actions are illegal and treasonous, and you still don't get to run the country even though you think you know better than the rest of us. Thanks again to the media for colluding in covering it up.

The mentality switched to fabricating a Russian collusion hoax, a non-existent Ukrainian corruption narrative, and a sham impeachment. None of which resulted in Democrats getting to run the country. I have always held the belief it's not really about hatred for Donald Trump. I have always held the belief that it's not really about hatred of Republicans or conservatives. It is becoming increasingly apparent that it is about a mentality that only leftists are smart enough and morally superior enough to run the country. And they will do it by any means possible, even when their power is not sanctioned through the election process. The will of the people be damned, they deserve to be ruling class and if necessary, they will pull the strings of power from behind the scenes through coups and elements of the deep state.

It was a good thing none of these tactics worked because Democrats have nothing to offer the country in the way of viable policies or candidates. And that is the reality of why the Democrats will be unsuccessful again in 2020, no matter what the media tells the people who live in the bubble. The truth of the matter is, that the "fake" impeachment changed the dynamics of the bases of each party, very little. In lieu of any significant crossover effect, the strategy for conservatives has to be to make the people who are planning to vote Republican aware of the extreme gravity of the next election, so that every one of them will get out and vote.

Nevertheless, the atmosphere will be one of intolerance. Only one point of view is acceptable. Opposition will not be tolerated. Conservative speakers are already banned from many college campuses. Conservative voices are to be harassed, restricted, and silenced if necessary.

"Few in this part of the Country Class have any illusion that retreating into private associations will long save their families from societal influences made to order to discredit their ways. Day after day the ruling class imputations,-racist, stupid, prone to violence, incapable of running things--hit like artillery cover for the advance of legislation and regulation to restrict and delegitimize.

There is no escape from the conflict between the classes." (The Ruling Class)

> "In the ramifications of Party doctrine...the principles of Ingsoc, doublethink, the mutability of the past and the denial of objective reality, and to use Newspeak words... In a way, the worldview of the Party imposed itself most successfully on people incapable of understanding it. They could be made to accept the most flagrant violations of reality, because they never fully grasped the enormity of what was demanded of them, and were not sufficiently interested in public events to notice what was happening....They simply swallowed everything, and what they swallowed did them no harm, because it left no residue behind, just as a grain of corn will pass undigested through the body of a bird." (George Orwell '1984')

HYPOCRISY

"Hypocrite: The man who murdered his parents, and then pleaded for mercy on the grounds that he was an orphan." Abraham Lincoln

This is where up is now down, right is wrong, and everything is upside down. It is a by-product of what Sean Hannity refers to as, a bifurcation of the brain. Bifurcation is a special ability of liberals to only see one side of any issue and to be able to not apply the same set of rules to two sets of circumstances.

George Orwell referred to it as, "Doublethink means the power of holding two contradictory beliefs in one's mind simultaneously, and accepting both of them."

Some examples;

It used to be that if you criticized a person of color you were a racist. Now if you compliment a person of color you are a racist.

Democrats supported slavery, gave rise to the Ku Klux Klan, the Black codes and Jim Crow and they call Republicans the party of racism.

America is portrayed as an evil and racist country when only 3.6% of slaves from Africa came here.

Liberals believe in the exceptionalism of the individual but not of the country.

Liberals believe that they can defy law and create sanctuary cities when it concerns immigration policy that they disagree with, but if conservatives want to create sanctuary counties in defiance of Second Amendment restrictions (as in the case of Virginia),they should be prosecuted.

Remember when Obama claimed that his administration was the most transparent ever and then he gave us the Hillary Clinton Foundation pay to play scheme, the fast and furious scandal, the IRS conservative targeting scandal, the Benghazi fiasco, the Joe and Hunter Biden conflict of interest quid pro quo scheme, the Clinton email scandal, the infamous Iranian nuclear deal, etc, etc., just to name a few. It turns out in retrospect that the perception of that transparency was only aided by the complicit news media and the truth is Obama's administration might have been one of the most corrupt.

When Biden brags on camera about withholding aid to Ukraine unless a prosecutor who is investigating his son is fired and the media sees no reason to investigate a quid pro quo.

Trump is accused of collusion with Russia and yet Obama is the one who was caught on a hot microphone telling the Russian ambassador that he would have "more flexibility" after the election.

Trump is accused of being a Nazi when it is the Democrats who use similar Nazi tactics when it comes to media and education.

Hillary Clinton bleach-bits her emails which were under a subpoena while Trump releases the transcript of his phone call to Ukraine and Trump is accused of obstruction.

The Trump family has to divest itself of business interests in order to get into politics when the Biden family uses politics to get into business.

When Obama was elected president, it was supposed to narrow the gap between race relations, but they only deteriorated.

The condition of minorities was supposed to improve under Obama and they only declined with higher unemployment and higher numbers on food stamps.

Liberals claim to care so much for our children and yet they are the ones that support partial birth abortion.

Democrats run an impeachment inquiry in the House that is completely biased and devoid of due process and then scream bloody murder when Republican in the Senate do the same thing.

Democrats in the House say it would take too long to subpoena witnesses in the impeachment inquiry and rush through the process claiming urgency because Trump is a clear and present danger and then after the vote Nancy Pelosi delays sending the articles of impeachment to the Senate.

Liberals proclaim environmental urgencies as they drive around in their gigantic SUV's and their private jets.

Liberals will tell you that walls are obsolete as they barricade themselves in gated communities.

Liberals will denounce gun violence and support gun confiscation as they are protected by armed bodyguards.

When Obama takes out a terrorist like Osama Bin Laden (something that was applauded by both sides of the aisle at the time) the victim is portrayed as evil; and yet when Trump takes out a terrorist Iranian military official, the victim is portrayed as a revered leader.

Nicholas Sandman a Catholic school student who did nothing but stand his ground in the face of being taunted is vilified by the press, while Jussie Smollett perpetrates a hoax that he is the victim of an attack and he is adulated by the press.

The news media who claim to be so concerned about the children who are separated from their family at the Southern border spike the Jeffery Epstein story on pedophilia enabling it to claim many more victims.

Legend in Your Own Mind (LIYOM) This category seems to be reserved for former vice presidents. Al Gore claimed he invented the internet and was responsible for leading the charge on climate change. Yet he owned multiple homes and would travel exclusively by SUV caravan and private jet.

Joe Biden was responsible for saving civilization from "Cornpop" and his gang and advised President Obama to pull the trigger on Osama Bin Laden when he is caught on tape in his own words advocating for just the opposite.

According to Joe Biden he was front and center on the issue of Apartheid in South Africa with Nelson Mandela who was imprisoned. Biden claims he was arrested as well but the problem is that no one can find any record of his arrest. Biden later walked it back and said he wasn't actually arrested but was 'prevented' from visiting Mandela and was 'separated' from his group. Only a LIYOM would equate being prevented from visiting someone with being arrested. And would it only make sense, that if he was with a group of black people that he might be separated at times because he was in an Apartheid country. It all sounds like a bunch of malarky.

The ultimate example of this kind of dissonance is how both sides of the aisle can look at the same event and both sides have opposing views.

Here is a real tale of two philosophies made even more contradictory when they are juxtaposed.

In the first scenario, a man assaults a police officer in New York City, knocking him to the ground and fighting with him until he is restrained and arrested. Under new legislation in New York, that loosens bail procedures, this perpetrator is back on the street before the police officer who was assaulted can even finish his shift. What kind of signal does this send?

In the second scenario, a man walks into the West Free Church of Christ in Texas, with 240 parishioners attending a service, pulls out a shotgun and begins shooting innocent people. Because of recent legislation in Texas, concealed carry permits are extended to public places with their consent as is the ability to have volunteer armed security if so desired.

The killer with the shotgun is killed by an armed parishioner six seconds after he guns down two people. Consider what the carnage would have been, if the people in this church had been at the mercy of this killer until police arrived. What kind of message does this send?

A SPECIAL KIND OF STUPID (ASKOS)

Hypocrisy is one thing, but some things rise to a much great level of stupidity.

After President Trump was impeached in the House of Representatives, many young people immediately went on social media to proclaim that Donald Trump was no longer our president.

"This is yet another example of how spectacularly our system of public education has failed.....But you have to a very special kind of stupid to actually think that Donald Trump is no longer our president...If much of the population actually thought that Donald Trump was no longer president because he was impeached by the House, what else can they be led to believe?" (Michael Snyder)

The answer to the question Michael Snyder poses is *anything.* Anything the left wants them to believe. Anything the leftist media wants to tell them. That was precisely the mission of the liberal controlled education system--to condition our youth to swallow whatever the left tells them and to be dumb enough to do it without question.

Let me give you an example of how this works.

The Democrat Party wants to protect one of its candidates running for president in 2020--Joe Biden.

The leftist media spouts the propaganda line that they want everyone to believe, that Joe Biden did nothing improper even though his son Hunter Biden was given positions in Ukrainian energy companies although he had absolutely no experience in energy.

Then the graduate of the education system who has no ability to analyze a situation that even a cursory examination would conclude that Hunter Biden was given lucrative deals because his father was vice president, take the media at its face value as they have been trained to do and believe that there was nothing going on here and go back to their politically correct video games. That is how the special kind of stupid enables Democrats to achieve political power.

What is disappointing in this process is that older liberals are also taken in by it. There are many liberal thinking people in this country who are smart, talented and successful people who are achieving great things and are for all intents and purposes are good people and they too would believe Joe Biden's statement that there was nothing untoward going on with his son.

One of two things is happening here, either they are so blinded by their hatred of Donald Trump that even though they can see the real truth in the Biden situation they still choose not to acknowledge it, thus they become a victim of TDS - Trump Derangement Syndrome. Or they are so immersed in this liberal Democratic party mainstream media conspiracy complicity of misinformation that they cannot discern fake news or truth, and once again that is a special kind of stupid.

When Biden brags on camera that he is withholding aid to Ukraine unless they fire a prosecutor who is investigating his son's questionable business ventures and the media sees no quid pro quo to investigate. That is a special kind of stupid.

The most important is the concept that Americans will sacrifice the well-being of the country for the power of a political party. That is a special kind of stupid. Conservatives in this country endured 8 years of Obama's ineffective leadership and policies but in most instances these same conservatives were not rooting for the country to fail.

When politicians and news media will look American citizens in the eye and knowingly lie with the sole express purpose of dividing the country and trying to overturn an election and the will 63 million Americans. That is a special kind of stupid.

When the goal of our education system is to turn our students into indoctrinated lemmings who will follow instructions without thinking or questioning. That is a special kind of stupid.

When people come to the United States and denigrate this country while glorifying the country they left. Another case in point. New Hampshire used to be a red state. The liberals from the blue state of neighboring Massachusetts didn't like the way that state was being run and the high taxes, so they began migrating to New Hampshire. Over time, New Hampshire was converted to a blue state. The same liberals who escaped Massachusetts then came to New Hampshire and transformed it into the same state they didn't like living in. This is a typical liberal phenomenon that can only be described as a special kind of stupid.

When we are condemning people "as disgusting human beings" for exercising their constitutional right to vote and erasing everything good that they have accomplished in their life based on who they voted for. That is a special kind of stupid.

Bernie Sanders appears to be the candidate who is benefitting the most by the planned obsolescence of our education system. He has accumulated a lot of support particularly by seducing young people because his message is custom-made for non-critical thinkers. He is proposing free education, free healthcare, climate change reform and a redistribution of wealth; all attractive issues in theory to a young person, no doubt. However if you delve below the superficiality of these programs you realize that nothing is free and the costs have to be borne somehow. What Sanders is proposing as his solution is at least socialism if not downright communism and those are systems that have failed everywhere they have been tried and have resulted in the deaths of millions of people. But young people won't question it because they have been rendered by our education system as a special kind of stupid. If Sanders is the Democrat nominee the election of 2020 will not only be a referendum on socialism vs capitalism but it will be a generational contest because Sanders has drawn the majority of his support from the young people of the country. It will be interesting to see if the left's strategy of taking the education system hostage will finally pay off.

After everything we have been through on 9/11, our flight schools continue to teach people of Mid-Eastern descent how to fly planes even though they are not interested in learning to land them. That is a special kind of stupid.

Not voting for a president with a proven track record and a roaring economy in favor of socialism. That is a special kind of stupid.

When during an inquiry a direct transcript of a conversation is available as evidence and Adam Schiff feels compelled to concoct a parody of what was really intended by the direct transcript. When Schiff was called out for his deception, he claimed it was just in jest— and yet not a single person thought it was funny. Now that is a special kind of stupid.

This is really when up is down

When Obama takes out a terrorist like Osama Bin Laden and there is not one single solitary objection form anybody in the country. We are unified. When Trump takes out a terrorist of similar import and HALF the country sides with the terrorist and the president who is protecting American lives is called a war criminal.

For the Iranian Ambassador to claim that Iran is not a lawless country is tantamount to Nazi Germany claiming that it is a trustworthy nation. When foreign countries are recognizing that they can say anything they want because half of America is too stupid to know the difference—we are in real trouble. That is an existential threat and that is a special kind of stupid.

DEEP STATE/ RULING CLASS ELITE

"In the councils of government, we must guard against the acquisition of unwarranted influence, whether sought or unsought, by the military-industrial complex. The potential for the disastrous rise of misplaced power exists and will persist." (Dwight Eisenhower, former president)

"As we know with the Dems, if they can't rule America, they will seek to destroy it. Causing total chaos is their next best option to resisting Trump's efforts to drain the swamp, since the Dems know they can't defeat Trump in an honest election." (m.beforeitsnews.com)

The deep state is just a method of keeping control of power when they are not officially in power.

"In sum our Ruling Class does not like the rest of America. Most of all it dislikes that so many Americans think America is substantially different from the rest of the world--and like it that way."

"Its first tenet is that its members are the best and brightest, while the rest of Americans are retrograde, racist and dysfunctional unless properly constrained. How did this replace the Founding Fathers' paradigm that 'all men are created equal'?" (from the Ruling Class.)

When you have convinced yourselves that you are the smartest people in the room, everyone else looks stupid in comparison; presidents notwithstanding.

Abraham Lincoln was portrayed as a country bumpkin, ridiculed for his "apelike" appearance, and even his intellect was disparaged while he was in office. It was only after his death that he was credited for his exceptional wisdom.

Ronald Reagan was characterized as just a stupid actor. Donald Trump was a reality tv show star.

On the other side, Jimmy Carter was praised for his wit and intelligence even though he was a product of rural America and Obama was hailed as an eloquent speaker of professorial intellect. It's funny how that doesn't quite translate into results for the country unless it was all another media-created bubble in the first place. Reagan and Trump will go down in history as having the best economies America has ever experienced, while the Carter and Obama administrations will be remembered as economic disasters. Carter presided over 21% interest rates, inflation, gas lines and failed military interventions. Obama accumulated more national debt than all the other presidents before him, combined.

However, Donald Trump has something in common with another president, that being JFK. They both distrusted the Deep State.

John Kennedy inherited a rather tenuous set of circumstances when he was elected into office. It would come to be known as the Bay of Pigs. Prior to the Kennedy administration, Cuba had been operating under the corrupt regime of General Fulgencio Batista, who was in league with organized crime syndicates in the United States. Batista was corrupt but he was also anti-Communist and supported by the American government.

When Batista was overthrown by a young nationalist named Fidel Castro, legitimate American business as well as the interests of organized crime were expelled from the island of Cuba. For the next two years, the Central Intelligence Agency and the U.S. State Department sought to remove Castro from power. In 1960, outgoing President Eisenhower approved the recruitment of 1400 Cuban exiles for a military incursion into Cuba. In May 1960, Cuba established relations with the Soviet Union.

In January 1961, the U.S. cut off diplomatic relations with Castro and escalated a plan for invasion. Kennedy assumed office in the midst of those preparations. Kennedy was conservative by many standards, certainly by today's, but at the time he was viewed as weak on the Cold War. It was an image that he wanted to dispel, and he saw this as an opportunity to set the tone right out of the gate.

However, he had doubts about the logistics of the plan, and he was adamant that it be a covert operation with no direct ties to America. He did not want to risk Soviet Union retaliation. Kennedy was assured by CIA officials that invasion would be a success and it would be clandestine.

The first indication that things might not go as predicted was when a strike against a Cuban airfield proved to be ineffectual, primarily because Castro had been warned. When the Cuban exile force landed on the beach at the Bay of Pigs, Castro's troops were waiting for them. Much of the success had relied on the element of surprise and when that was blown, 1100 exiles were taken prisoner. Kennedy had air support on standby but in the end he refused to commit those forces.

The debacle of the Bay of Pigs was a huge embarrassment for the Kennedy administration. Never again would Kennedy trust the CIA or the National Security Council. Kennedy would subsequently fire CIA director Allen Dulles, cut the agency budget by 20% and was contemplating dismantling it altogether. He confided to an aide that he would "splinter the CIA into a thousand pieces and scatter it to the winds." (Philip Shenon, 'A Cruel and Shocking Act')

Kennedy crossed swords with other deep state entities. It was rumored that he was considering pulling American forces out of Vietnam completely-- a potentially huge loss of revenue for the military industrial complex. It also extended the notion that Kennedy was weak on Communism and this ran contrary to the war hawks in the deep state. His policies were not in alignment with theirs.

In many ways he was the disrupter of his time, refusing to follow the traditional protocols of governance and the powers behind the curtain did not like to be left out of the loop. JFK made his brother

Robert his attorney general and his trusted confidante to the exclusion of others in his administration. Kennedy was a rebel in a sense and the establishment saw him as an existential threat to their power. Thus he had to be neutralized. It is my contention that that is the WHY Kennedy was assassinated. It was their way of controlling the power from behind the curtain--like a puppet-master.

At about 12:30 pm Dallas time on November 22, 1963 a man stands on the sidewalk just below the grassy knoll in Dealy Plaza holding an umbrella. The sun is out; there is no rain in the forecast; no reason for anyone to be carrying an umbrella. As the limousine carrying President Kennedy draws level with him, the man with the umbrella inexplicably opens it up. Almost instantaneously gunshots begin to ring out. People in the crowd begin running or throwing themselves on the ground. In contrast the man with the umbrella stands calmly upright and folds up the umbrella. It's as if he knows who the intended target is and that he is not in the line of fire. It is the presidential limousine that has entered the killing zone. Simultaneously, back in the motorcade Vice President Lyndon Johnson ducks down in his seat. It's as if he also knows who the intended target is but he is a little closer to the line of fire and does not want to take the chance of getting hit with a stray bullet.

The bullets fulfill their mission. The final fatal shot may have been fired from the grassy knoll from a Remington XP 100 Fireball which is designed to fire ordinance that explodes on contact. Kennedy's head is shattered and he dies shortly thereafter.

It is the successful culmination of a coup d'état of a president of the United States and the beginning of the greatest hoax the Deep State has ever perpetrated on the American people. Lee Harvey Oswald is arrested a few hours later. He is accused of killing Officer Tippett and suspected of assassinating President Kennedy. He has a pistol on him and his fingerprints are found on a rifle discovered in the Texas Schoolbook depository where shots at the motorcade emanated. He claims he "is a patsy".

It is determined that his pistol has not been fired recently because it has a broken firing pin. He is given a paraffin test that detects recent gunpowder residue and that comes up negative. For a man who was supposed to have killed two men and fired multiple shots in the last few hours, the tests indicate that he has not even fired a gun that day. In a little over forty hours he will be dead as well, silenced forever. The Deep State had successfully planned, executed and covered up the removal of the President of the United States because he posed a threat to their interests. The ensuing Warren Commission Report was just a manipulated whitewash of the facts to cover up the conspiracy. To this day not a single person has been held accountable for Kennedy's death outside of Oswald and the evidence is increasingly in favor of him being set up. The Deep State has prevailed.

Donald Trump campaigned on a slogan and a promise that he would "Drain the Swamp". I still have one of those posters and at the time I never realized how prophetic it would be. Trump was never part of the "beltway". He financed much of his campaign with his own money. He was never indebted to special interests.

He declined to take a salary after he was elected. He was never beholden to the corrupt nature of interests in Washington and that is what the establishment feared most-an outsider. He was about to become their worst nightmare. And he would get it from all sides.

The Washington Post printed an article that called for Trump's impeachment within 20 minutes of his inauguration. However, the resistance was initiated even *before* he got into office.

Maybe even far earlier than that. I remember watching a debate between Mitt Romney and Barack Obama during the 2012 election. Obama looked totally unprepared for the debate and Romney really took him to task in what was a dismal performance for the normally well-spoken Obama. Obama was also coming off of 4 years in office, in which he had not accomplished many results for the American people-- certainly not a record that would inspire confidence in re-election.

And yet the very next day after that debate, Obama was giving interviews like he had won the debate. He wasn't the least bit fazed by his poor performance. He still had that air of smugness about him, like it didn't matter what he did, the result was still in the bag. It appeared to me as if he *knew* that he was not going to lose.

I often speculated about that. Was the synchronization of education, media, Democrats and the Deep State so arrayed against Republicans even that far back, that a Republican victory was almost an impossibility? We know now that it was nothing less of a miracle for Republicans to have prevailed in 2016. There is evidence that a coup against Trump was in the works during his campaign and resulted in the Russian collusion hoax.

The Inspector General Horowitz report concluded that there was a conspiracy of officials within the FBI, CIA and State Department, that used a unverified Steele dossier that they knew was false. It was paid for by Hillary Clinton to unlawfully deceive a FISA court into obtaining a surveillance warrant against an American citizen--one Carter Page. Carter Page was associated with the Trump campaign and in effect, it was a window in which this cabal of the deep state could use to spy on a presidential candidate.

I personally fail to see how a break-in at a DNC office in the Watergate hotel to obtain information on Democrat Party operations was so prosecutable that dozens of people went to jail and the illegal surveillance has been glossed over, at least to this point in time. At the very least, it was evidence of a cabal of deep-staters within the government, trying to effect a coup d'état against a duly elected president. The more profound implications are that a group of elitists who did not like the outcome of an election are trying to suborn the will of 63 million voters.

All of it would never have come to see the light of day if Hillary Clinton had won the 2016 election and the country would be well on its way into the darkness of 1984 Orwell by now. Authors like Gregg Jarrett, "The Russia Hoax" and Lee Smith, "The Plot Against the President" have exposed the involvement of the deep state in much greater detail.

"The term 'Deep State' originated in the Middle East, describing the human bedrock of hard-security regimes,...managed by an entrenched network in which the military and security establishment intersect with political and corporate interests."

'They're educated suburbanites, many with law degrees. They exchange tips about curling and grilling meat, drink craft beers and text their girlfriends on their way home to put their children to bed and kiss their wives goodnight. They share state secrets with journalists in exchange for basketball tickets....The journalists who could have exposed the plot went to the same parties as the spies." (Lee Smith, "The Plot Against the President")

The Deep State is vague, it shadowy, but it's *real*. Look no further than the biased now infamous emails between Lisa Page and Peter Strzok, who not only worked together but were having an affair.

Page " ...you're meant to protect the country from that menace." [Trump]

Strzok "I can protect our country at many levels."

Page "Trump is a loathsome human."

Strzok "Omg he's an idiot."

Page "He's awful."

Strzok "God Hillary should win 1000000-0..."

There's no way he gets elected-but I'm afraid we can't take that risk. It's like an insurance policy in the unlikely event that you die before you're 40..." (Greg Jarret, 'The Russia Hoax')

Not long after, operation Crossfire Hurricane was launched to spy on Donald Trump.

The latest resistance 'flavor of the week' is the Ukrainian phone call that has resulted in impeachment in the House of Representatives--the Democrat controlled House of Representatives. The resistance is all about Trump Derangement Syndrome and knows no bounds.

Case in point: During the recent Trump impeachment hearing GOP representative Mike Turner asked Gordon Sondland the US ambassador to the EU: "No one on this planet told you that this aid (to Ukraine) was tied to investigations. Yes or no?"

Sondland: "Yes."

Sondland said that he was only "presuming" that it was. His only direct evidence was "his presumptions."

Turner: "And that's nothing."

Can you imagine anyone going into a court of law trying to convict somebody on their 'presumptions' never mind trying to use that as evidence to impeach a sitting president of the United States.

That's how bad the Deep State wants to get rid of Donald Trump and how infected they are by their own Trump Derangement Syndrome.

"...if they can't rule America, they will seek to destroy it. Causing total chaos is their next best option..." (m.beforeitsnews.com)

TENETS
(FROM THIS BOOK THAT YOU CAN TAKE TO THE BANK)

America has to be taken down. (destroyed)

Whatever a liberal accuses you of doing, they are guilty of doing it themselves.

Liberals believe that for something to be true or factual, all they have to do is proclaim it.

Liberals are specialists at creating captive audiences. (schools, airports, news outlets)

Liberals can dish it out far better than they can take a punch.

Except for a few exceptions, the news media is the propaganda arm of the Democratic Party.

Liberals are always the smartest people in the room and they know everything about everything.

Liberals should be running the country.

According to the left, Conservatives are "bitter", "smelly Walmart shoppers" who "cling to God and guns".

DEPENDENCE = CONTROL = POWER

The left does not care about our children.

The left does not care about minorities.

The left does not care about the Constitution and its laws.

The left does not care about our country.

The left cares about political power above all else. (they will use any group, employ any tactic, sacrifice anything to achieve power).

NEW WORLD ORDER

"You can vote Communism in, but you will have to shoot your way out." (Facebook meme)

This is where the rubber meets the road. This is where it all came together for me, not really as an epiphany but as a series of trial and error experiences, questioning and applying some critical thinking, to where I was able to assemble all the pieces of the puzzle, until they fit--or at least made sense to me. There was not really an "aha" moment, unlike my Kennedy revelation which I describe earlier, in that 50 years of examination and research had culminated in a transcendent moment when I visited the assassination site.

In contrast to the Kennedy situation, I was much more of a pawn in the perpetration of the education myth. I actually worked for the Department of Education for many years even though to them, I was just another a piece on the system's chessboard, one of many that they had successfully bamboozled and manipulated. Until there was a point, when I had what I would call an awakening. I puzzled for a number of years over the DOE's policies and modus operandi. A lot of the things they did seemed to run counter-productive to what should be expected of an educator in the teaching profession. Why are they not teaching our kids American values, to be independent, to be more analytical in their way of thinking? I kept banging my head against the wall until eventually the lightbulb came on.

THEY DON'T WANT TO. It is part of their *design*.

Only then did it begin to make some sense. I'm sure that there are a lot of people who get into teaching who have good intentions as I did. However, they are being played as I was and they haven't figured it out yet or they have figured it out and they are content to go along with the program, perhaps because they bought into the program long before they became a teacher.

It was never *my* program and so I was always a skeptic. Some thought I was just jaded, but it was more than that. I was unconvinced, resistant and defiant. The question I kept asking myself, became my gold standard.

To what end?

When I applied this question, the answers started to come, so I kept applying it. It is especially helpful when you take the forty-thousand foot view and scope out the whole landscape. So let's do that. Let's go up in the plane and do an exercise in IFTTT, (If this, then that).

Why is the system not teaching our kids traditional American values? *To what end?* So that they can replace them with a more leftist agenda.

Why is the system not teaching our kids to think critically? *To what end?* So that they will not be able to think independently, and they will accept what leftists tell them and accept it without question.

Why does the education system want to produce malleable students who have been exposed to left wing values? *To what end?* So that they will become malleable citizens predisposed to left wing values.

Why do they want to transfer the microcosm they have created in the classroom to the laboratory of society? *To what end?* Because it translates to power. The power they hold over the educational system will be Democratic political power in the public sector. A herd of sheep predisposed to left wing values, dependent on Democratic socialist handouts and shepherded by a corrupt and complicit media is an easily controlled and formidable voting bloc. And ultimately a pathway to power. Power is always the ultimate goal. Power trumps everything.

Here is the formula that encapsulates the leftist road to achieving power.

INDOCTRINATION+DEPENDENCE=CONTROL= POWER

I like to characterize the leftist world view versus the conservative world view in this manner. Let's say you have two cats; one is a domesticated house cat and the other is a wild feral cat. The feral cat is out in the wild, hunting and foraging for its survival. It is not dependent on anyone and it is free to hunt when, what and where it wants. No one controls it therefore no one has power over it. It enjoys its natural God-given freedom.

The house cat, on the other hand, is dependent on its masters for food, water, shelter and medical care. It enjoys no freedom and is a "captive" (it's funny how this word keeps popping up when there is a reference to the left) in its artificial environment. It has become accustomed to the illusion of security, but it is wholly at the mercy and the benevolence or the malevolence of its master.

And the cat had no say in the choosing of its master. It is dependent on the master for the basic necessities of life. The master controls its destiny, therefore the master has the power of life and death. If the domesticated cat were to seek its freedom in the wild, it would most likely die because it doesn't have the natural ability that it was born with, to survive.

Is this not an adequate analogy of the incestuous education, media, Democratic Party, socialism symbiotic relationship? One feeding off the other.

Couple cases in point. Recently Democratic presidential candidate Kamala Harris proposed a ten hour school day. It caused a modicum of controversy at the time it was announced. Rebecca Friedrichs was interviewed as opposing this measure. She has been a strong advocate against teachers' unions purportedly because they do not have our kid's best interests at heart. Her argument is that more time at school is just more time to brainwash our kids, make them completely dependent on the State for meals, medical, what they will learn, and make their parents irrelevant in the development of their lives. I agree with her and I saw this firsthand as a teacher in New York City. We had very few snow days because the school was everything--even babysitter--and parents were at a loss about what to do with their own kids if they were not in school. And that's what the school is intending to be—surrogate parents. The nanny state. From morning, noon to night. They are essentially striving to be glorified babysitters. And they don't even do a good job at that. They make great dysfunctional babysitters.

When Barak Obama was elected president in 2008, people of color and Democrats were delirious, and they had a right to be. He was the first black president. I was a little more reserved in my judgement and it had nothing to do with skin color. I knew very little about the man. Just a few years before he was a relatively unknown community organizer and had come out of nowhere to be elected president of the United States. It seemed to be such a precipitous ascent in such a short period of time. I also wanted to see him in action before I graded his work. There was no doubt that he was an eloquently spoken man, but words are one thing and deeds are another. Let's see what he does.

A few weeks into his administration, somehow, he won a Nobel Peace Prize. I'm not sure even he knows to this day what he did to justify it. How could anybody produce a body of work in a matter of weeks that was significant enough to be worthy of such a prestigious award? Others have worked lifetimes for such an honor. Now I began to get suspicious.

Four years later I knew everything that I needed to know, and it had nothing to do with skin color. The US economy was in dismal shape, our deficit and national debt were sky-rocketing and our military was in one of its weakest state of affairs, despite being involved in conflicts all around the globe. Just on that record alone, one could have safely assumed that this was going to be a one term presidency. But this president still talked a good game--good enough to get re-elected in 2012.

At this point, I began applying my gold standard litmus test again. To every policy that Obama tried to enact, I measured it against the question--"Is this the best thing for the country?" The only thing that ever passed the test was the assassination of Osama Bin Laden. On virtually every other issue from declining the XL pipeline at a time when we were in need of both energy and jobs, to sending billions of dollars to Iran when we were in debt and Iranians were screaming "death to America" as they were developing nuclear capabilities, Obama seemed to be on the other side. In fact, completely on the other side, like 180 degrees on the other side.

President Obama always impressed me as being a fairly intelligent man but some of these proposals were of breath-taking stupidity. Not even a special kind of stupid does it justice. So what is any rational human being left to conclude? The only thing they can conclude in the face of such evidence:

IT WAS INTENTIONAL.

How can I say such a thing? That an American president was intentionally trying to sabotage the country from within. It is not such a hard preposition when we go back to the 40,000 foot view and look at the scenery from a global scope and ask our question again "To what end?"

America is the biggest obstacle to globalism. Other countries have opened their borders to a flood of immigrants, have adopted socialistic, environmentalist policies and anti-nationalistic principles. America has continued to cling to its founding principles of freedom and capitalism, but barely by its fingernails. God forbid, if Obama had retained control of the House and the Senate during his second term in office. They were the only checks and balances that prevented him from wreaking complete havoc on our country and the Constitution at the time. But not to worry, they had Hillary Clinton waiting in the wings to finish the job. It was all rigged so that she would assume the throne and continue the transformation of America. How else do you explain the predetermined primary with

Bernie Sanders and the superdelegates? Many people say she stole the nomination.

And how do you explain the fixed investigation on Hillary with her illegal private server and her bleached-bit emails? Emails that had been under subpoena. The same people who were in on the exoneration fix of Hillary Clinton were the same people who were generating a Russian collusion hoax against Donald Trump. The Jim Comeys, the Peter Strzoks and the Lisa Pages of the world. And how do you explain Bill Clinton meeting with attorney general Loretta Lynch on an airport tarmac while his wife was under an investigation? If that is not a conflict of interest and the appearance of impropriety, I don't know what is. All this to what end? Because it is impossible for anyone to rule the country from a jail cell.

But then something happened.

The problem was that, against all odds, something, nothing short of a miracle, shocked them to their core. They lost the election. The plan to take America down from the inside was derailed, at least temporarily. And make no mistake about it, America *has* to be taken down in the globalist scheme of things. America must be diminished for globalism to be fully implemented. It is too much of a beacon of light.

It explains why the reputation of America is constantly tarnished and denigrated. America was regarded as the greatest country in the world, but we are not perfect. To be honest, we have made mistakes in the past, but many mistakes were in the context of the times. The rest of the world was doing the same thing, or in many cases, far worse. And yet Barack Obama felt compelled to go on an apology tour in his first term as president.

Immigrants are taught to hate this country even as they seek to come here to live and to take refuge. It really is an amazing phenomena. They will risk their lives to come to our shores and enjoy the benefits of our economy and our freedom and then in the same breath, they use their freedom to condemn us and idolize the place that they just escaped from. It truly is a sight to behold. They don't appreciate our country and they don't respect our laws and they don't make any attempt to assimilate.

Congresswoman Ilhan Omar is a perfect example. She was in a refugee camp in her country and her life was in extreme peril. She was granted asylum and came to the United States. We offered her safety, financial support and freedom. She parlayed that into political power, which would have been unthinkable in her home country and yet she is a prominent voice in the castigation of America.

Leftists want to flood this country with immigrants because it changes the demographics in their favor and increases their chances of political power. Because of the left's policies it has become MORE advantageous to be an immigrant than a citizen. Through their various policies and proposals it is now or will be possible for an illegal immigrant to have a previous deportation reversed and have his legal expenses and inconveniences paid for by the American taxpayer. (The New Way Forward Act.) The illegal immigrant can get free housing, welfare benefits, free medical care, free college tuition, social security, a driver's license, and can't even be arrested if they are stopped by police and they don't have a driver's license (Cambridge Massachusetts). Boston conservative talk show host Howie Carr is famous for his plea, "I don't want any special treatment, I just want to be treated like an illegal immigrant." He's right. Immigrants are acquiring more rights than citizens under a liberal agenda. Why wouldn't an immigrant want to come here? It's like they're throwing chum in the water. Is it any wonder why the country is becoming more and more polarized?

We are constantly lectured (a specialty of leftists in general and Obama in particular) about how America should try to emulate Europe. The last time I looked Europe wasn't doing that well with high unemployment, inflation and plenty of immigration consequences. Why would we want to emulate those failed policies unless we wanted to replicate the same kind of detrimental results?

We are told that we must align with global protocols regarding the environment. America's leftist Green New Deal must be implemented or we are facing extinction in 12 years. However, it has been revealed that some proponents of this scare tactic admit that this course of action is less about saving the environment and more about the distribution of wealth. America must be taken down.

"While the Ruling Class prods Americans to become more like Europeans and talks as if Americans should move up to 'world standards' the Country Class believes that America's ways are superior to the rest of the world's and regards most of mankind as less free, less prosperous and less virtuous than American." (The Ruling Class)

By contrast, say whatever you want about Donald Trump, but one thing is indisputable--that he loves the United States of America and he puts the country first. He passes the gold standard test--"what is best for the country?" and again, say what you want about his style, but the results have been nothing less than spectacular. His economy might be the best in the history of the country.

At one point during his campaign, Trump criticized the Obama administration for their loss of manufacturing jobs to companies overseas and claimed that if he was elected president he would reverse this trend. Obama condescendingly alluded, that this was the new normal and derided Trump by saying "what was he going to do, wave a magic wand?" Maybe in lieu of a wand, all Trump really needed was the *desire* to do something that was in the best interests of the country.

Donald Trump has thrown a giant unexpected monkey wrench into the gears of the globalist machinery. And this is becoming more evident with each passing day. The election of Donald Trump has exposed the true nature of the Democrats, the media, and the deep state for the rest of the country to see. The America, as the sovereign traditional country that we once knew, was on life support, before Trump got elected and he almost single handedly resuscitated it.

He has rolled back the globalist agenda far more than they would have ever expected. Trump is their worst nightmare. And that is why there is such hatred for him. It is called Trump Derangement Syndrome and it is attributed to the Democratic Party in America because he defeated them in the election. How can there be such hatred for a president who is achieving such unprecedented positive results for the country? The left has even extended their hatred to include all conservatives and anyone who ever voted for Trump.

Honestly, I think that Trump Derangement Syndrome is just a cover for the movement of globalism. He is an obstacle in their path of a new world order and so are the people who support him and voted him into power. He stands in their way. Conservatives stand in their way. And an America in the control of Republicans stand in their way.

The 40,000 ft view starts with education and ends with globalism. In between, the plan is to demonize Trump, demonize his supporters and bring down America. Some say the plan doesn't end there and it goes beyond globalism. Listen folks, I never claimed to be a genius or a prophet or have any special skills of divination. I'm just an ordinary guy who was an educator for 15 years teaching history. But I've also been around long enough to know when it feels right. And this fits. Only when the pieces of the puzzle are put together in this manner it does seem to make sense. It was just like the Kennedy experience that I had. It all went together and made sense--at least to me. That's the scheme in a nutshell. Sometimes you need to read between the lines. Sometimes you don't need all the details. Sometimes you just know a thing is right.

What is this globalism anyway? This new world order? This one world order? It all seems very vague to me. When I start hearing those terms, I start imagining some kind of 1984- esque, soulless, desolate society, of dependence on government, with Big Brother as the totalitarian leader, I guess. Maybe my concept is not that far off. To me, 1984 paints about as bleak a picture of society as I can imagine-- and yet let us not forget that it is based on actual conditions under Fascism and Communism, regimes that exist in places today. By all rights we should all be speaking German to each other right now. Most of us in this country will never know how close we came to that reality. My grandfather emigrated from Hungary with his family in the nineteen thirties, because he sensed that Hitler's rise to power would not have a good outcome. He had fought in WWI in the German army and his son (my father) would fight against Germany in WWII. My father always said that Germany was the most powerful military force in the world at that time (but as a kid I found it hard to accept that America could be defeated.) However, he was right. Germany could have faced any other country in the world and would have defeated them in a one to one confrontation. Germany made the fatal mistake of taking on too many countries at one time and Hitler's betrayal of Stalin drove the Russians over to the Allies. Even with that it was still touch and go and Hitler very nearly realized his dream of world domination. However in the end America prevailed. To me Nazi Germany and 1984 are almost the same thing, the latter is only an evolutionary version of the former. However, one thing I am certain of is that the light of America is the only thing that stands between us and the darkness of that world.

When they extinguish that light--God help us all.

I mean that literally. There are people who take this to a higher level, a spiritual level--one of prophecy. And end times prophecy does not include any prominent mention of the United States of America.

It does mention a powerful antichrist.

And an Armageddon.

LEFTIST FLOW CHART AND TIMELINE

- Infiltrate higher education with leftist ideology
- Infiltrate public education with liberal educators and administrators
- Indoctrinate students with liberal propaganda
- Remove God from public education
- Remove traditional values from public education
- Replace parents with the state
- Do NOT teach students how to think as individuals
- Infiltrate Democratic Party with the Leftist agenda
- Enlist the media in the Leftist propaganda campaign
- Coordinate Democratic Party and media resources to coerce a predisposed voting block to achieve political power
- Indoctrinate citizens with liberal propaganda
- Remove God from the country
- Replace God with environmentalism.
- Remove traditional values from the country
- Replace individual liberty and responsibility with dependence on the state
- Institute socialism
- Use environmentalism to instill fear in Americans to adopt its precept when its real goal is not to protect the environment but as a scheme for the distribution of wealth

- Destroy America as a world power and sovereign nation
- Erase all borders and boundaries between, individuals, sexes and countries
- Revel in globalism

Phase I—take over education
Phase II—indoctrination of the younger generations
Phase III—enlist media to perpetrate propaganda
Phase IV—gain political power
Phase V—create chaos
Phase VI—destroy (in lieu of political power)

SCENARIOS

"A house divided against itself cannot stand, I believe this government cannot endure,...but I do expect it will cease to be divided. It will become all one thing or all the other." (Abraham Lincoln)

There is a preface to this section that must be considered before we delve into *how* it could happen and that is *what* could happen. In the first Civil War, the technology of warfare was at the cutting edge of the time. Most of the physical battles were fought on the confederate territory of the South. The cities of the South were devastated--rendered virtually uninhabitable--the human carnage was unprecedented.

The second civil war will not be so kind. Our technology for destruction is far beyond the capacity of what was even imaginable in 1860. We possess the annihilation capability of nuclear armaments. There is the possibility that some of the combatants of one side or the other will be able to survive, declare victory and establish a ruling government. Unless we engage in some kind of limited warfare, the question at that point will be

"Will there be anything left over which to rule?"

The following circumstances are determined by the precipitating event, the instigator and the probability of occurrence.

Scenario #1

The Democrats win the 2020 election. If conservatives feel that it was a fair election they might abide by the decision of the electorate, but they will never respect or allow a Democrat president to govern without constant resistance. It is the new norm that has been established by the Democratic treatment of President Trump. The Democratic resistance has severely damaged our Constitution and I'm not sure that it can be repaired in a way to allow us to function as a Republic going forward. If a Democratic administration were to start implementing leftist policies such as socialism that would destroy a vibrant economy or gerry-rigging the election demographics in a way that would make it impossible for a Republican to ever win an election in the future--it might be enough to trigger civil unrest. Taking away the rights of citizens results in loss of freedom. Probability of a civil war-- moderate.

Scenario #2

Donald Trump is re-elected in 2020. The pattern of resistance by the Democrats and 'fake news' by the mainstream would continue unabated. The question is whether they would ramp up their attacks enough to mobilize widespread protests and demonstrations. Also, if liberals were to continue to widen the scope of their attacks to include all conservatives, it would continue to set up a dangerous dynamic of--us versus them. I think the likelihood of civil unrest depends entirely on just how aggressive the left wants to get, because the right will not tolerate much before they fight back. The left will be the instigator. The likelihood of a civil war--moderate.

Scenario #3

"The ballot is stronger than the bullet." (Abraham Lincoln)

Donald Trump is prevented from re-election in 2020. If Donald Trump and by extension the 63 million people who voted for him in 2016, are denied the constitutional right to a free and fair election in 2020, the repercussions will be immediate. Anything but a free and fair election will be the death knell of freedom in this country. Our elections are one of the major elements that sets us apart from other countries. Conservatives have already witnessed the disintegration of other institutions of our Republic. They will not tolerate this. If there is any perception by conservatives that the election was stolen from them, there will be a civil war. Conservatives will be the instigator. The probability of civil war--high.

Scenario#4

Donald Trump is unjustly removed from office. If President Trump is prematurely removed from office for any reason, by any means that is deemed by conservatives to be unjust, before the 2020 election--it will be perceived by the right wing of the country to be sabotage. The repercussions will be immediate. The instigator will be conservatives. The probability of civil war--high.

Scenario #5

Secession: Conservative views don't mesh with liberal views--they run contrary There is no common ground. We are countryman and we don't even like each other. Most of us can't sit at a table and have a meal or a drink without acrimony. We call each other names and harass each other in public places. We take the same event and have two completely opposite versions of what happened. How can that be? Intimidation and violence have begun and will only escalate.

Sanctuary cities and threats of secession already divide us. Our differences run deep through families and are irreconcilable. We need to divorce to avoid escalation and inevitable civil war. It is time to call it a day on the United States of America as we knew it. The sooner we recognize the fact the union is over and accept it, the sooner we can begin to engage in joint bi-lateral mediation and terms of separation. The Union has failed but we have preserved our freedom to live as we see fit with like-minded citizens. Probability of civil war--low to none. What will secession look like?

Secession

"In great contests each party claims to act in accordance with the will of God. Both may be, and one must be wrong. God cannot be for, and against the same thing at the same time." (Abraham Lincoln)

For all intents and purposes, psychologically we already have become two America's in the same physical space that we used to be recognized as united states in one sovereign country. The result of this is a fundamental transformative change in the makeup of our society.

A conservative has distinct characteristics: guns, religion, probably lives in middle of the country and is a "deplorable Walmart shopper." Conservatives are pro-military, pro-law enforcement and against government regulation and intrusion into their personal lives. A liberal is a socialist-minded, environmentalist, self-professed elitist who lives in a coastal city. Liberals are pro same-sex marriages, rainbow coalitionists and want to tear down our border walls. These are just some of the ideologies of each side and there is no common ground whatsoever. Can anyone tell me that there is one scintilla of compatibility in these two stances?

Each side thoroughly detests each other. Couples are breaking up over these differences. Husbands and wives are disagreeing in fundamental ways. Our differences are becoming so profound and consuming, that holiday family gatherings are turning into physical brawls over politics. Where have we seen such a rift become so pervasive and consuming before? There answer is, it was the *last* time America hosted a civil war. We are realizing with every passing day that these differences are irreconcilable.

In the past a Democratic or Republican designation was just that, a political identification. Half the time there was no discernable difference between the two and it did not matter much who was in power because the governance was largely the same. We used to be Americans with two or more political choices. We were all citizens under one American roof, and we wanted the best for our house. That concept does not apply any longer.

Our political parties have evolved and now they are representative of not only distinct ideological and views but distinct ways of life. And each of the two major parties has become not just representative but imbedded with each of the divergent lifestyles.

Our differences will only get worse, if that is possible. The old saw that 'opposites attract' might have some truth to it, but they don't *stay* together. In practicality diversity doesn't work. Studies have shown that the longest marriages are successful because the partners have more things in common. Diversity doesn't work. We need to separate. Diversity is our enemy. We need to get a divorce.

Physically, we are already beginning to separate. What else would you call sanctuary cities? They have already made declarations to defy federal laws. Is that not in essence, a declaration of independence? Liberals are concentrated in the coastal cities, and some of these areas have already contemplated outright secession. Some would say that we are already two countries within one. Canada is an example of a country that went through this phase. The French provinces primarily Quebec, wanted to secede back in the 1970s. The majority of Canada is of British heritage. The French minority felt that because of their language and cultural differences they had less say in their governance and were in danger of losing their identity.

There were demonstrations and protests that escalated into violence and killings. The federal government was forced to make concessions in order to appease French Canadians. One of these, was to adopt two official languages, at a great expense to the taxpayers, which in some ways didn't make sense to the English-speaking provinces. However, it cannot be denied that the conciliations avoided further violence, but there is still a lot of resentment and even today many consider Canada, a country of two nations. But they are at peace.

America is already two countries in one. Why not just make it official? If secession had been allowed to stand in 1860, I contend that it might have avoided civil war. One can only surmise what kind of country would have evolved. It would have been interesting to see how the institution of slavery would have fared if it had not been abolished when it was. There is no doubt that secession is a drastic measure but no more drastic than the existential threat that civil war poses.

This time secession won't be along North and South lines at the time of the civil war, designated by the Mason-Dixon Line. This time it should be East and West. The demarcation line should run from the Gulf of Mexico north along the eastern borders of Texas, Oklahoma, Kansas, Nebraska, South Dakota and North Dakota all the way to the Canadian border.

Anything west of that line becomes liberal territory and everything east of that line becomes conservative territory. We could call it 'Westamerica' and 'Eastamerica'. That gives the libs California and Texas and the entire border with Mexico. At that point if they want to implement their open border policies--they can choose to tear down the wall. If conservatives want to insulate themselves from that decision, they can build their own wall from the Gulf of Mexico, north to the Canadian border.

At that point we would be two separate entities. If we had made the determination that we couldn't live in peace together, maybe we could find a way to live in peace, alongside each other. We would essentially be neighboring countries. At that point, liberals in the east would have to settle their estates and move to the west and vice versa. Perhaps a property transference or exchange program could be set up. The two separate entities would implement their own systems of government and establish their own societies based on their own values. If they wanted to interact or continue trade relations, those would be individual decisions of each sovereignty.

If nothing else, it would be the ultimate greenhouse experiment. One side would embrace the principles of the original American experiment and the other side would be free to pursue all the principles of socialism, open borders, sanctuary cites, free Medicare for all, the green new deal, free college education, and 75% tax rates. You know, all the things the Democrat Party stands for now. Wait a minute—isn't that the exact same choice that we have in the next election? I have a funny feeling that if we did implement this secession experiment, it wouldn't take long before the wall between Westamerica and Eastamerica would have to be a lot higher in order to keep the people from Westamerica from trying to get out.

On the surface secession may sound like a rather extreme and far-fetched proposal. But it has always been an option lurking behind the scenes of a union of individual states. It bubbled up after our war with England and once again before the Civil War. It has shown its face in liberal states such as California. More recently it is being discussed among conservatives in Idaho who want to take parts of California and Oregon and form their own conservative state of Greater Idaho.

"Rural counties have become increasingly outraged by the laws coming out of the Oregon Legislature that threaten our livelihoods, our industries, our wallet, our gun rights, and our values, " Mike McCarter, one of the chief petitioners, said in a news release. "We tried voting those legislators out, but rural Oregon is outnumbered and our voices are now ignored. This is our last resort."

"Ultimately this is yet another sign of how incredibly divided we have become as a nation. In recent years we have seen multitudes of conservatives move to red states and multitudes of liberals move to blue states, and that trend is likely to accelerate in the years ahead.

It has gotten to the point where many of us literally do not even want to live in an area that is controlled by the other side, and the 2020 election is going to deepen our existing political divisions no matter who ends up winning." Michael Snyder

Maybe the idea of secession is not such an outlandish idea after all, but at least something to consider.

As Donald Trump once asked the black community before the 2016 election,

"What do we have to lose?"

Of course, if we found out that we couldn't co-exist under this configuration, we could always resort to that old tried and true solution--that the world has relied on for thousands of years.

We could always go to war.

THE PATH OF MOST RESISTANCE

"In waging a scorched earth, no-holds-barred war of 'Resistance' against this Administration, it is the Left that is engaged in the systematic shredding of norms and the undermining of the rule of law." (Attorney General William Barr, Federalist Society, Nov 2019)

Trump Announces his Candidacy in the 2016 Presidential Election June 16, 2015

Trump announces his candidacy while descending an escalator with his wife, Melania. Trump's many critics believed his campaign would not go very far.

Trump's populist, nationalist campaign, which promised to "Make America Great Again" and opposed political correctness, illegal immigration, and many free-trade agreements, garnered extensive free media coverage...The tone of the general election campaign was widely characterized as divisive and negative. Trump faced controversy over his views on race and immigration, incidents of violence against protestors at his rallies, and numerous sexual misconduct allegations including a controversial tape. Clinton led in nearly every pre-election nationwide poll and in most swing-state polls, leading some commentators to compare Trump's victory to that of Harry S. Truman in 1948 as one of the greatest political upsets in modern

U.S. history. (2016 United States Presidential Election, Wikipedia, 11/8/16)

Calls for Impeachment Begin January 20, 2017

Representative Maxine Waters calls for impeachment on Trump's inauguration day. "Impeach 45" she chants.

The effort to remove duly elected President Donald Trump dates back to the day he was inaugurated, first announced in a *Washington Post* article dated January 20, 2017 titled, "The Campaign to Impeach President Donald Trump Has Begun" and it included a video of six protestors at the inauguration hoisting a "Resist" banner. The *Post* reported on the start of what has been an almost constant effort to take Trump down by the left. (*Breitbart,* by Penny Starr, 12/18/19)

"In May of 2017, Texas Rep. Al Green became the first Democrat in Congress to support impeaching President Donald Trump." *Buzz Feed* reported. "Trump had, at the time, been in office for just four months." (*Breitbart*, by Penny Starr, 12/18/19)

May 16, 2017 CNN – CNN host Wolf Blitzer brought up the possibility of impeaching President Trump in an interview with Senator Angus King (I-Maine) Tuesday evening after a *New York Times* article alleged the president asked then-FBI Director Comey to end the FBI investigation of former National Security Advisor Michael Flynn.

July 12, 2017 – *The Hill*. Rep. Brad Sherman (D-CA) formally introduced an article of impeachment against President Trump on Wednesday that accuses the president of obstructing justice during the federal investigation of Russia's 2016 election interference.

Nov. 2, 2017 – *The Mercury News*. Tom Steyer's campaign has gathered steam: In 14 days, his petition calling for Trump's impeachment has gathered more than 1.4 million signatures. His 60-second ad – which is playing nationwide on TV and online – argues that Trump has "obstructed justice" and "brought us to the brink of nuclear war," as video rolls of North Korean President Kim

Jong-un. It has been viewed nearly 1.2 million times on YouTube and 474,000 times on Facebook

Dec. 6, 2017 – *National Public Radio.* Texas Democrat Al Green forced a House vote on the impeachment of President Trump on Wednesday, but a broad bipartisan majority voted down the effort.

Jan. 19, 2018 – *GovTrack.US website.* "On Motion to Table: H. Res. 705: Impeaching Donald John Trump, President of the United States, of high misdemeanors." The vote was to kill a resolution impeaching President Donald Trump. It was the second vote on impeachment since the President took office.

Special Counsel Investigation of Alleged Collusion Between Russia and the Trump Campaign May 2017 – March 2019

The investigation concluded that Russian interference to favor Trump's candidacy occurred "in sweeping and systematic fashion", but "did not establish that members of the Trump campaign conspired or coordinated with the Russian government." (2016 United States Presidential Election, Wikipedia, 11/8/16)

Media Stares Down 'Reckoning' After Mueller Report Underwhelms, by Michael Calderone, *Politico*, 3/24/19. "The Mueller [report] concluded no one from Donald Trump's 2016 presidential campaign "conspired or coordinated" with Russia in attempting to influence the election has ramped up scrutiny of the news media's handling of the two-year investigation. "The 3 biggest losers from the Mueller report in order – the media, the media, the media." *Tweeted National Review* editor Rich Lowry. It's not only prominent conservatives, the president's TV boosters and family members calling out the media, but also some journalists on the left who have long been skeptical of the Trump-Russia story. "If there's no media reckoning for what they did, don't ever complain again when people attack the media as 'Fake News' or identify them as one of the country's most toxic and destructive forces," wrote the *Intercept's* Glenn Greenwald."

Inspector General Horowitz's Report on Alleged Abuses of the Foreign Intelligence December 2019

What Horowitz Actually Debunked by Daniel Henninger, *The Wall Street Journal*, 12/11/19. "Within minutes of the 434 page report's release Monday, the generic media headline was that it "debunks" the idea that the FBI was guilty of political bias against Mr. Trump, as well as conservatives "conspiracy theories" that there was a deep-state effort to get Mr. Trump….Thousands of news stories appeared through this period suggesting myriad, concrete Trump campaign linkages to Russia. It is more than a little insulting to the intelligence of the average person to straight-facedly write now that this massive media output based on Beltway leaks was not for a moment about trying to damage the Trump presidency. But let us agree: If something is running off the front pages virtually every day of the week, it's not a conspiracy… the report is mind-boggling, shocking and damning. It is page after page – indeed, paragraph after paragraph-detailing gross errors of judgement and violations of FBI investigation protocols…The report notes that besides the seven significant errors in the first October 2016 [FISA] application, the three renewals in 2017 had "10 additional significant errors," including this: that (1) Steele's reporting was going to Clinton's presidential campaign and others, (2) Simpson was paying Steele to discuss his reporting with the media, and (3) Steele was "disparate that Donald Trump not get elected and was passionate about him not being the U.S. president."

Trump Impeached December 18, 2019

Trump impeached for "abuse of power and obstruction of Congress" based on claims by Democrats that Trump tied military aid and a White House meeting to Ukraine publicly announcing investigations into former Vice President Joe Biden and his son Hunter Biden. At the same time, Democrats turn a blind eye to evidence shown repeatedly on a video of Joe Biden bragging "In 2006

Ukrainian Prosecutor General Viktor Shokin, in his investigation of corruption involving Burisma Holdings, a natural gas company, identified Hunter Biden as the recipient of over $3,000,000 from the company. Not wanting his corruption exposed, Joe Biden swung into action, using US loan guarantees as hostage while demanding Shokin be fired. Amazingly, Joe Biden brags about his actions in this matter. Joe Biden was supposed to announce another billion-dollar loan guarantee to Ukraine when he stated that he would not give the loan guarantee unless the prosecutor investigating Burisma was fired within 6 hours. The prosecutor was indeed fired within the allotted 6 hours. The real "quid pro quo." *YouTube* video *"Joe Biden Brags about getting Ukrainian Prosecutor Fired."*

The President's Best Ukraine Defense: Not an Impeachable Offense, by Andrew C. McCarthy, *National Review*, 10/27/19. "It is certainly fair to contend that, in the absence of some vital, emergent American interest, a president should not put a hold on aid to a friendly and strategically significant nation that Congress has directed in legislation and the president himself has signed into law. The Constitution, however, gives the president sweeping foreign-affairs authority, so Trump would arguably have had the power to decline to deliver the aid altogether. This, by contrast, was merely a temporary delay that was of no consequence to Ukraine's defense. If we were talking about any other president, some criticism would be in order. To portray what happened as an impeachable offense is just the next stage in a tireless political campaign. It trivializes impeachment."

Trump and Negative Media Coverage

Media Trump Hatred Shows in 92% Negative Coverage of His Presidency: Study -*Investor's Business Daily,* 10/10/18. Anti-Trump Media: To say that the big networks haven't exactly had a love affair with Donald Trump, as they plainly did with President Obama, is an understatement. A new survey shows that not only is coverage of Trump overwhelmingly negative, but the president's biggest accomplishment – the roaring economy – gets almost no attention. For its report, the Media Research Center did a lot of visual spadework. It viewed some 1,007 evening news stories about the Trump White House on ABC, CBS and NBC from June 1 to Sept. 30. That's the equivalent of about 32.7 hours of coverage, by TV standards and eternity of news time. What they found was, as Trump himself might say: "Over the summer, the broadcast networks have continued to pound Donald Trump and his team with the most hostile coverage of a president in TV news history – 92% negative vs. just 8% positive."

Trump is Popping in the Polls by Brian C. Joondeph, *Rasmussen Reports, Commentary.* "Watch most cable or network news shows and the message is clear – President Donald Trump is unpopular, especially compared to the dozens of fresh faces attempting to challenge him for the White House in 2020….Despite the exonerating Mueller Report, Trump is still on the ropes, about to be impeached, a Russian agent, and so on. Trump is also a Nazi, racist, homophobe, Islamophobe, and sexist pig. Nobody likes him. At least that's what CNN says. If that was truly the case, Trump should be polling in the low 30s at best, with most of the country giving him and his administration a thumbs down on performance and results. Yet reality is far different. In the media bubble, where journalists all live in the same neighborhoods, kids attend the same schools, all go to the same parties and belong to the same tennis and fitness clubs, there are no MAGA hats to be seen. Outside the bubble, the picture is far different, even if the smart set at MSNBC and the *New York Times* choose not to see it…*Rasmussen*, in their daily presidential tracking poll as of Friday, April 5, President Trump had a 51 percent total approval number. Most of the calendar year, despite the constant drumbeat of Russian collusion, his approval number has been in the mid to high 40s, ranging from a low of 43 percent to a high of 52 percent since January 1."

Inside the Media's Relentless Crusade to Destroy President Trump, by Kimberley Strassel, *New York Post*, 10/13/19. "Since Donald Trump's election in 2016, the mainstream media has shed its once-noble mission – the pursuit of the truth – and instead adopted a new purpose: to take down the president…The press has embraced its bias, joined the Resistance and declared its allegiance to one side of a partisan war. It now openly declares those who offer any fair defense of this administration as Trump "enablers." It writes off those who question the FBI or Department of Justice actions in 2016 as "conspiracy" theorists. It acts as willing scribes for Democrats and former Obama officials; peddles evidence-free accusations; sources stories from people with clear political axes to grind; and closes its eyes to clear evidence of government abuse. This media war is extraordinary, overt and increasingly damaging to the country."

The relentless onslaught of Democratic resistance that has resulted in manufactured hoaxes and coup d'états from within the government and directed against a duly elected president has destroyed the trust in our institutions of this country for the foreseeable future. It has set a precedent that has damaged our constitution beyond repair. Does anyone think that after what has been done to this president, that Republicans will do any less to the next Democratic president? Our system of governance has been hamstrung. Is this the way we want to hobble into the future. We have abdicated our responsibilities as stewards of our Constitution. Together we have squandered our Republic. The Republic as we knew it is over. It is time for us to separate and go our own ways.

ESCALATION PHASE

59% of anti-Trumpers will turn violent if Trump is re-elected. Rasmussen poll 11/22/ 19

"If we don't stop (President Trump) now, then we will have a revolution for real. Then there will be blood in the streets." James Cromwell actor Carney awards October 2018

The rhetoric is rising. The signs are disturbing but not unpredictable.

Democrats are urged to get in the face of their political opponents.

"Let's make sure we show up wherever we have to show up. And if you see anybody from that Cabinet in a restaurant, in a department store, at a gasoline station, you get out and you create a crowd. And you push back on them. And you tell them they're not welcome anymore, anymore." (Representative Maxine Waters at the Wilshire Federal Building)

Maga (Make America Great Again) hats are now offensive and are enough to spark violence.

Then of course there is Antifa. They claim to be the militant branch of the left-wing who are opposed to fascism and other forms of right-wing ideology. For a group that is supposed to be anti-fascist, it is surprising how reminiscent their tactics are of the Brownshirts of another infamous fascist regime in Germany.

The caravans from South American countries were not what they seemed to be on the surface. Democrats were not always for open borders as they are now. They recognized then as conservatives do now that open borders are a surefire pathway to the destruction of a sovereign country.

When Democrats realized that unchecked immigration changed the demographics of elections by creating a dependent constituency in their favor, they were suddenly all for it. It fits the pattern. They are willing to sell out the country for political power. But changing demographics takes time, however flooding the border with unprecedented masses of illegal immigrants has a much more immediate impact. These caravans were not a random collection of refugees who gathered together on a whim. They were part of a concerted effort to recruit and organize them into massive caravans. They were funded and assisted by liberal entities on their journey through Mexico. They were advised not to seek asylum in Mexico but make America their goal. Their assault on our southern border was nothing short of an invasion that completely overwhelmed the resources of our law enforcement. As a result, there were deplorable conditions and there were deaths. Democrats may not have created any immediate voters, but they created escalating tensions. And immediate chaos.

Homelessness is prevalent in liberal run cities such as Los Angeles, San Francisco, Chicago and New York. It is almost as if Democrats are cultivating it by encouraging lawlessness because they want a dependent constituency and they want the chaos.

Virginia. The situation in Virginia has the potential to escalate into a point of ignition. It is one thing to put restrictions on types of weapons, magazine capacities, bullet configurations and background checks even those things may well be unconstitutional, but when liberals venture into gun confiscation territory that is a horse of a completely different color. The last time a Democratic politician (Beto O'Rourke) tried to ride the gun confiscation pony he vanished over the horizon faster than Clint Eastwood in Pale Rider.

Some citizens will no doubt surrender their guns without much resistance but for the majority of gun owners you are infringing on their right to defend themselves and their freedoms. If you have read this book to this point and knowing what we know about liberals, why would we ever consent to allowing leftists to disarm us without a fight? It is the equivalent of suicide for conservatives. That is exactly what they have in mind and what is playing out in Virginia.

For those who are not familiar with the situation, Virginia has passed some state laws that will restrict gun ownership and take effect in 2020. Most of the counties in Virginia have declared themselves 2A sanctuary counties and will decline to enforce these new laws much like liberal sanctuary cities defy immigration laws. The governor has declared that these laws will be enforced, and strict measures will be employed if necessary, such as calling in the national guard and setting up roadblocks. Some suggest that this is an attempt to force the issue. It appears that martial law is also a possibility, but at the very least a chaotic situation is in the making.

"Virginia's Democratic politicians appear to be ready to drive the state into a period of massive civil unrest with no regard for citizen's wishes, but conservatives in the commonwealth will not be stripped of their rights without a fight." (Western Journal.com)

This could be the flashpoint.

This is our future. This is what it will look like. This is what is coming down the pike.

Confiscation of arms will trigger civil unrest.

Corruption of a free and fair election process will trigger a civil war.

There is a distinction to be made between the 2016 election and the 2020 election. In 2016 the Democrats thought they had it in the bag. They didn't know what hit them. They never saw it coming. Since that election, it has been a series of orchestrated resistance directed at Trump. It started with the Russian collusion hoax, the creation of the border crisis and the organized caravans, the Kavanagh debacle, the contrived Ukrainian corruption phone call, and the illegitimate impeachment. The Democrats have no problem putting this country through needless acrimony and further dividing it. It is their plan. They know full well that if things continue on their present course the only surprise of 2020 will be the size if Trump's victory. It is a foregone conclusion.

That is not something that Democrats can permit. We have already seen what the Democrats are willing to put the country through for their political power. This is about to escalate in my estimation. We know that they are willing to destroy the country if necessary. It only remains to be seen what price they will demand America pay.

Finally the ultimate kicker in all of this which might serve as the epitome of the hatred of the left for the rest of us, (as if what has preceded this isn't chilling enough), is this little article. It comes from Metro reporter Jimmy McCloskey who quotes Denver Democrat Councilwoman Candi CdeBaca, "For the record, if I do get coronavirus I'm attending every MAGA rally I can." Think of the magnitude of this. This is a woman in public service whose commitment to elected office should be the well being of her fellow citizens and instead has promised to intentionally infect them with a serious disease that has sickened and killed thousands of men women and children worldwide. This is what she as an elected public servant of the American government wishes to inflict on her constituents and her fellow countrymen and her nation. They really do want to kill us.

AMERICAN LYNCHPIN

Trump is as much of a lynchpin as Washington or Lincoln were. Trump is the central character of this work--everything revolves around him and yet I found it ironic that the essence of this book was completed on the very day that Trump was impeached in the House of Representatives 12/18/19.

When I got to this section of the book, I wondered if my estimation of President Trump would be the same as when I started writing it. It has changed. I think that Trump is underappreciated and his accomplishments are under-estimated. I don't think that Trump gets enough credit for what he has endured and what he has achieved in a relatively short time in office. I think that a regular politician, without the extraordinary pain threshold that Trump must possess, would have crumbled under the weight of this relentless resistance. I think that Trump deserves to be given his due diligence. That was not the intent of this book at its conception. Its intent was to illustrate the significance of his office in the context of the precarious disposition of the country in recent times. But like a lot of things it has evolved, and in many ways, writing this book has proven to be cathartic for me.

In the process, although I would never presume in any way to equate the import of our respective situations, I discovered a lot of similarities between the two of us. In the course of writing this book, I almost developed a kinship with Donald Trump.

We both came out of the private sector to work in public service. We didn't take the job for money or security. In fact, it was a risk and a sacrifice that neither of us *had* to make, especially at that particular time in our lives--but we saw it as an adventure in life's journey. We were motivated by a desire, to make a contribution to the collective good, to make things better and we were driven by a feeling that we had something to offer. We both admire hard-working people and respect taxpayer money. We both love America and want it to be a place of success, for all of its citizens. We both challenged the status quo and know what it is like to go up against the power of establishment and feel the full weight of that wrath when it comes down on you.

Neither one of us could keep our mouths shut.

In my case, if I had just kept my mouth shut, kept my opinions to myself, never dared to question the tenets of the party line, and genuflected every time the king went by--I would have had a job for life. But I couldn't do that. I owed a responsibility to the parents who entrusted the education of their children to me, and to the taxpayer money that paid my salary. I was not about to break a covenant with the public trust and feed at its trough. It wouldn't have been the right thing to do and in the end, that's the metric I have to live with.

Donald Trump, on the other hand is the ultimate disrupter, the likes of which we have never seen before, but he is doing it on the behalf of the American people and his love of the country. He fights for us and his plan is to put America first and make it the best it can be.

We send our politicians to Washington to serve the people of this country, and so many of them only use their power to enrich themselves or entrench their party. The good of the country should always "trump" the political power of the individual or the party. And Trump is doing exactly that. He is taking on the establishment. Donald Trump is a street fighter and sure, he is rough around the edges, but he is the perfect man for the job of draining the swamp. He is the one that does the dirty work.

Do you think that is an easy job, the kind of job that requires Marquis of Queensbury rules? Are the swamp creatures going to surrender their cushy corrupt positions and go easily into that good night? Hell no! They are going to fight tooth and nail with every molar they have. It takes an equally tough and smart man to endure what he has encountered and to fight back.

He has already exposed a lot of political corruption and the collusion of the mainstream media with the Democrat Party.

In return, he has had to endure constant resistance in the form of a "fake" Russian collusion investigation, for three years, a "fake" Ukrainian corruption scandal, even a "fake" impeachment and yet that has not stopped him from continuing to work on behalf of the American people and keeping his promises.

And besides enduring the resistance he has had to undo many of the failures of the Obama administration before he could implement his own programs. For example, legislation on the economy and healthcare had to be repealed and then reformed. Many of the current problems he faces were a result of Obama's incompetence. Case in point: Iran. Obama cut a deal with Iran and dropped 150 billion dollars on an airport runway in the middle of the night(transparently of course) in an attempt to bribe the Iranians out of their nuclear weapon development program. Not only did the Iranians ignore the terms of the nuclear agreement but they continued their aggression against the world. Because of the Obama appeasement, Trump has to clean up the mess.

In light of that, his accomplishments are remarkable, and I felt compelled to list them at the end of this section. His work ethic and constitution in the face of opposition appears to be indefatigable.

President Trump has truly earned the designation of American lynchpin. He is truly a central, pivotal figure on the national and international political landscape. He is the only thing that stands between Democrats and Republicans. He is the firewall keeping back the tide of what is looming on the horizon--the tyranny of socialism and globalism. He is positioned squarely between liberalism and the conservative values of free enterprise, individual responsibility, a belief in God, exceptionalism, a strong work ethic, the Constitution and the spirit of freedom--values that this country was founded on and that have made it great. He is the only thing that is keeping the country from civil unrest.

Trump will never get the credit he is due because of his style, which many say is crude and undignified. But he has shown the conservative movement that it is ok to push back. He has emboldened conservatives and more and more of them are beginning to follow his example. He has led the right into the fray and has shown us the way. It is my conclusion that history will view him much more favorably. Based on what he has already achieved, his legacy will be as the greatest president ever in the history of the United States.

And also the last.

The only thing that is certain is that" the next election will be a battle for the soul of the country."

"We are not enemies but friends. We must not be enemies. Though passion may have strained, it must not break our bonds of affection. The mystic chords of memory will swell when again touched, as surely they will be, by the better angels of our nature." (Abraham Lincoln)

"My concern is not whether God is on our side, my greatest concern is to be on God's side, for God is always right." (Abraham Lincoln)

My hope in writing this book is that we as a nation can put our faith in God and pray for His guidance.

America is the spirit of freedom.

America is the light of the world.

We are America.

With God's help, we must not let them extinguish the Light of the World.

FINAL WORD AND LAST CALL

Liberals are professionals within the body politic. They are single-minded and organized, if they are anything. They will bring voters to the polls in busloads, if necessary. They are well-funded and it has paid off. Over the last 50 years they have fronted an organized assault on our institutions with their persistence and relentlessness. Whether insidiously or explicitly they have pervaded our bastions of American fundamentals and eroded out traditional values.

They have expunged God from our schools and the public square. They are in control of the education system. They are destroying our families. They have circumvented the Constitution and eroded our freedoms. They have selectively ignored some laws and enforced other laws. They have co-opted the press and corrupted the political system. They are trying to confiscate the Second Amendment (right to arms) and nullify elections (right to vote.)

Their ultimate endgame is the acquisition of power.

To my conservative brethren, when is enough enough? When *all* our rights are gone it will be too late. Our problem is that we have never been a united force on the same page.

Conservatives are busy with their jobs and raising their families.

"The Country Class is not anti-government, just non-governmental. It views the way people live their lives as the result of countless private choices rather than as the consequence of someone else's master plan." (The Ruling Class)

Conservatives are not all consumed by politics. If some of us do not like an aspect of one of our candidates, we do not show up at the polls. A perfect example is Mitt Romney. Some Republicans did not like his religious affiliations, so they chose to stay home. That can no longer be the way conservatives view elections. There is no perfect candidate-they are all flawed in one manner or another.

But the alternative is much worse. It is total eradication of traditional America as we once knew it. I keep coming back to the phrase, "The next election will be a battle for the soul of the country". I don't know if Joe Biden coined it, but he was one of the ones who recently proclaimed it. Joe Biden is not a poster boy for being on the right side of the issue over the last fifty years, but on this topic, he has never been more right in his life. What is coming if conservatives lose this next election, is a tidal wave that will wash over this country and totally transform the landscape like not even George Orwell could have imagined. We are facing a totalitarian society of 1984. That will be our cold, sterile reality. The 'experiment' will have failed. The world will have come full circle to a time before there was an America. And that might be the *best* scenario we can hope for. I can't even begin to imagine anything beyond that.

Is that the future you envision for yourself and your children? Only one thing stands in the way of a total abduction of our freedoms and that is the American Lynchpin of our time--Donald Trump. Now is not the time to stand on the sidelines. It is time to come forward and take a stand. EVERY conservative must stand with him. He has shown us the way. It is time to push back. If you are not with us you are against us. It can be framed in no other way. It is that critical. It is the LAST call. It is now or never. I implore my fellow countrymen, that if you care about this country, if you care about your freedom.

Stand up NOW!

Keep on rockin' in the free world.

"FREEEEEEEEEDOOOOOM"

President Trump's Accomplishments since his 2016 election
Almost 7 million jobs created since election.

- More Americans are now employed than ever recorded before in our history.
- We have created more than 400,000 manufacturing jobs since his election.
- Manufacturing jobs growing at the fastest rate in more than THREE DECADES.
- Economic growth last quarter hit 4.2 percent.
- New unemployment claims recently hit a 49-year low.
- Median household income has hit highest level ever recorded.
- African-American unemployment has recently achieved the lowest rate ever recorded.
- Hispanic-American unemployment is at the lowest rate ever recorded.
- Asian-American unemployment recently achieved the lowest rate ever recorded.
- Women's unemployment recently reached the lowest rate in 65 years.
- Youth unemployment has recently hit the lowest rate in nearly half a century.
- Lowest unemployment rate ever recorded for Americans without a high school diploma.
- Under Donald Trump's Administration, veterans' unemployment recently reached its lowest rate in nearly 20 years.
- Almost 3.9 million Americans have been lifted off food stamps since the election.
- The Pledge to America's Workers has resulted in employers committing to train more than 4 million Americans. We are committed to VOCATIONAL education.
- 95 percent of U.S. manufacturers are optimistic about the future—the highest ever.

- Retail sales surged last month, up another 6 percent over last year.
- Signed the biggest package of tax cuts and reforms in history. After tax cuts, over $300 billion poured back in to the U.S. in the first quarter alone.
- As a result of our tax bill, small businesses will have the lowest top marginal tax rate in more than 80 years.
- Helped win U.S. bid for the 2028 Summer Olympics in Los Angeles.
- Helped win U.S.-Mexico-Canada's united bid for 2026 World Cup.
- Opened ANWR and approved Keystone XL and Dakota Access Pipelines.
- Record number of regulations eliminated.
- Enacted regulatory relief for community banks and credit unions.
- Obamacare individual mandate penalty GONE.
- Trump's Administration is providing more affordable healthcare options for Americans through association health plans and short-term duration plans.
- Last month, the FDA approved more affordable generic drugs than ever before in history. And thanks to our efforts, many drug companies are freezing or reversing planned price increases.
- We reformed the Medicare program to stop hospitals from overcharging low-income seniors on their drugs—saving seniors hundreds of millions of dollars this year alone.
- Signed Right-To-Try legislation.
- Secured $6 billion in NEW funding to fight the opioid epidemic.
- We have reduced high-dose opioid prescriptions by 16 percent during his first year in office.
- Signed VA Choice Act and VA Accountability Act, expanded VA telehealth services, walk-in-clinics, and same-day urgent primary and mental health care.

- Increased our coal exports by 60 percent; U.S. oil production recently reached all-time high.
- United States is a net natural gas exporter for the first time since 1957.
- Withdrew the United States from the job-killing Paris Climate Accord.
- Cancelled the illegal, anti-coal, so-called Clean Power Plan.
- Secured record $700 billion in military funding; $716 billion next year.
- NATO allies are spending $69 billion more on defense since 2016.
- Process has begun to make the Space Force the 6th branch of the Armed Forces.
- Confirmed more circuit court judges than any other new administration.
- Confirmed Supreme Court Justice Neil Gorsuch and nominated Judge Brett Kavanaugh.
- Withdrew from the horrible, one-sided Iran Deal.
- Moved U.S. Embassy to Jerusalem.
- Protecting Americans from terrorists with the Travel Ban, upheld by Supreme Court.
- Issued Executive Order to keep open Guantanamo Bay.
- Concluded a historic U.S.-Mexico- Canada Trade Deal to replace NAFTA.
- Reached a breakthrough agreement with the E.U. to increase U.S. exports.
- Imposed tariffs on foreign steel and aluminum to protect our national security.
- Imposed tariffs on China in response to China's forced technology transfer, intellectual property theft, and their chronically abusive trade practices.
- Net exports are on track to increase by $59 billion this year.
- Improved vetting and screening for refugees, and switched focus to overseas resettlement.

- We have begun BUILDING THE WALL. Republicans want STRONG BORDERS and NO CRIME. Democrats want OPEN BORDERS which equals MASSIVE CRIME.

A Leftist Manifesto for Control of the Masses (based on the playbook of the Third Reich)

Education

Purge the school system from college professors to public school teachers of any educators who espouse a dissenting or opposite viewpoint.

Erase the events of past history that don't fit the narrative.

Allow for a period of time in order that people will forget what really happened.

Rewrite or modify history to fit the narrative and only teach that version. Repeat this for all subjects in the curriculum.

Remove any references to God and especially Christianity from the classroom.

Replace religion with the state or the environment.

Discourage or ban any free speech or opposing voices.

Get children into the system as early as possible and keep them as long as possible.

Make the school the state-the be all end all that children and their parents become dependent on.

Supplant the parents as the authority in the children's lives.

Do not let children become critical or independent thinkers. Discourage creativity and individualism of any kind.

Place the highest value on conformity and teach them to obey and follow like sheep-without question.

Teach them to make decisions based on emotions-not reason or logic.

Pretend that you care about them.

Media

Completely disregard any previous mandates to present the public with the truth.

If there is no evidence to support your narrative--fabricate it--if and whenever necessary as long as it advances your agenda.

Ban or eliminate any dissenting viewpoints.

Promote your political agenda.

Only present one side of the story in the best light possible.

Society

Enlist other segments of society to support your agenda such as teachers' unions, government officials, Hollywood actors, music stars and youth organizations.

Create a culture that is sympathetic to your interests and in conjunction with a complicit media, bombard the masses from all sides with your message. This is called synchronization.

Erase as many boundaries as possible, including race, gender and sovereignty to create a uniform mass that is more malleable and much easier to control.

Government

Become the political entity that embodies your particular culture and promote from within those segments of society.

Coordinate support from the other elements and use your power to destroy any opposition.

In order to stay in power by any means possible make more people dependent such as illegal immigrants and promise all kinds of free programs.

Impose the blueprint for the education system on the general public.

Pretend that you care about the country.

Deep State

Hide the fact that you are really running the country with your money, the power you have accrued through the people you control, and the policies you exact in accordance with your agenda.

Subvert, undermine or eliminate any elements that run counter to the primary agenda. Use any means necessary.

Deny any theory of the deep state, its existence, or its intrusion even though there is evidence to support it.

We Liberals Must--Proviso

We Liberals Must--Allow the people of the country to elect the people who will govern the country. Any undermining of the process through improper impeachment or manipulation of election protocols, or by any other means, is disenfranchising 63 million Americans of their right to vote. This would set a precedent of the most dangerous consequences.

We Conservatives Must--Proviso

We Conservatives Must-- not trust the mainstream media until they demonstrate that they are capable of upholding their obligations to report the truth in a responsible and objective manner. Truth equates to freedom. "The truth will set you free".

We Conservatives Must-- not trust our leftwing education system to educate our children.

We Conservatives Must--turn out in force an re-elect President Donald Trump in 2020 as he is the lynchpin between our past and our future. He is the only thing that stands between us and the tidal wave that will wash away our freedoms.

We, The People Must-- Proviso

We, The People Must-- protect our election process if we want to preserve our country. It is the cornerstone where our freedom rests. It is what millions of Americans have given their lives to ensure. This has never been so evident as in 2020.

We, The People Must--not allow the process to be derailed by unjustified impeachment of a president or misconduct of fair election practices.

We, The People Must-- hold our press to their mandate which is to report the truth and inform the American Public in an objective manner so that they can make educated decisions to maintain our freedoms.

We, The People Must-- never give up our second amendment to bear arms.

We, The People Must--ask ourselves what sets our country apart. It is our freedoms. The freedom of speech, of religion, of the press, our right to vote, our right to equal protection under the law-all of which are enumerated in our Constitution.

We, The People Must--ask what is left that hasn't been corrupted?

The mainstream media(press) has completely abdicated their responsibilities to accurately and objectively report the truth.

Freedom of religion is under assault, especially Christianity.

Freedom of speech is also under attack, especially on college campuses.

Our justice system is being accused of being two-tiered and having unequal applications when it comes to Democrats and Republicans.

The Constitution is being rendered impotent and is in danger of breaking down.

The only institution left that gives us any sense of hope and integrity as a free country is our elections. It is the final bastion and if we lose that we lose our country as we know it. We will be no different than a third world banana republic.

We, The People Must--recognize when our differences are irreconcilable.

We, The People Must-- make a peaceful separation.

We,

The People Must-- at the very least give this our consideration.

WORKS CITED

Burrows, Edwin G. *Forgotten Patriots.* New York: Basic Books, 2008.

Carlson, Tucker. *Ship of Fools.* New York: Free Press, 2018.

Chaffetz, Jason. *The Deep State.* New York: Broadside Books, 2018.

Codevilla, Angelo. The Ruling Class. New York: Beaufort Books, 2010.

Friedrichs, Rebecca. *Standing Up to Goliath.* New York: Post Hill Press, 2018.

Hartman, Andrew. *A War for the Soul of America.* Chicago: The University of Chicago Press, 2015.

Hughes-Wilson, Colonel John. JFK An American Coup D"Etat. London: John Blake Publishing, 2013.

Jarrett, Gregg. *The Russia Hoax.* New York: Broadside Books, 2018.

Larsen, Erik. *In the Garden of Beasts.*

Levin, Mark R. *Unfreedom of the Press.* New York: Threshold Editions, 2019.

Malkin, Michelle. *Open Borders Inc. Who's Funding America's Destruction?* Washington DC: Regnery Publishing, 2019

McCourt, Frank. *Teacher Man.* New York: Scribner, 2005.

Meacham, Jon. *The Soul of America.* New York: Random House, 2018.

O'Reilly, Bill. *The United States of Trump.* New York: Henry Holt and Company, 2019.

Orwell, George. *1984.*

Philbrick, Nathaniel. *The Last Stand.* New York: Penguin Group, 2010.

Shaara, Michael. *The Killer Angels.* New York: Ballantine Books, 1974.

Shenon, Philip. *A Cruel and Shocking Act, The Secret History of the Kennedy Assassination.* New York: Henry Holt and Co., 2013.

Smith, Lee. *The Plot Against the President.* New York: Center Street, 2019.

Time-Life Books, Chicago: 1983.

Watson, Robert P. *The Ghost Ship of Brooklyn.* New York: Da Capo Press, 2017.

White, Theodore. *The Making of the President 1960.* New York: Barnes and Noble Books, 1961.

APPENDIX A

Excerpt from David McCollough Jr. commencement speech

No commencement is life's great ceremonial beginning, with its own attendant and highly appropriate symbolism. Fitting, for example, for this auspicious rite of passage, is where we find ourselves this afternoon, the venue. Normally, I avoid clichés like the plague, wouldn't touch them with a ten-foot pole, but here we are on a literal level playing field. That matters. That says something. And your ceremonial costume shapeless, uniform, one-size-fits-all. Whether male or female, tall or short, scholar or slacker, spray-tanned prom queen or intergalactic X-Box assassin, each of you is dressed, you'll notice, exactly the same. And your diploma but for your name, exactly the same.

All of this is as it should be, because none of you is special.

You are not special. You are not exceptional.

Contrary to what your trophy suggests, your glowing seventh grade report card, despite every assurance of a certain corpulent purple dinosaur, that nice Mister Rogers and your batty Aunt Sylvia, no matter how often your maternal caped crusader has swooped in to save you...you're nothing special.

Yes, you've been pampered, cosseted, doted upon, helmeted, bubble-wrapped. Yes, capable adults with other things to do have held you, kissed you, fed you, wiped your mouth, wiped your bottom, trained you, taught you, tutored you, coached you, listened to you, counseled you, encouraged you, consoled you and encouraged you again. You've been nudged, cajoled, wheedled and implored. You've been feted and fawned over and called sweetie pie. Yes, you have. And, certainly, we've been to your games, your plays, your recitals, your science fairs. Absolutely, smiles ignite when you walk into a room, and hundreds gasp with delight at your every tweet. Why, maybe you've even had your picture in the Townsman! And now you've conquered high school…and, indisputably, here we all have gathered for you, the pride and joy of this fine community, the first to emerge from that magnificent new building…

But do not get the idea you're anything special. Because you are not.

The empirical evidence is everywhere, numbers even an English teacher can't ignore. Newton, Natick, Nee…I am allowed to say Needham, yes? …that has to be two thousand high school graduates right there, give or take, and that's just the neighborhoods. Across the country no fewer than 3.2 million seniors are graduating about now from more than 37,000 high schools. That's 37,000 valedictorians… 37,000 class presidents… 92,000 harmonizing altos… 340,000 swaggering jocks… 2,185,967 pairs of Uggs. But why limit ourselves to high school? After all, you're leaving it. So think about this: even if you're one in a million, on a plant of 6.8 billion that means there are nearly 7,000 people just like you. Imagine standing somewhere over there on Washington Street on Marathon Monday and watching sixty-eight hundred yous go running by. And consider for a moment the bigger picture: your planet, I'll remind you, is not the center of its solar system, your solar system is not the center of its galaxy, your galaxy is not the center universe. In fact, astrophysicists assure us the universe has no center; therefore, you cannot be it. Neither can Donald Trump… which someone should tell him… although that hair is quite a phenomenon.

"But, Dave," you cry, "Walt Whitman tells me I'm my own version of perfection! Epictetus tells me I have the sparks of Zeus."

And I don't disagree. So that makes 6.8 billion examples of perfection, 6.8 billion sparks of Zeus. You see, if everyone is special, then no one is. If everyone gets a trophy, trophies become meaningless. In our unspoken but not so subtle Darwin competition with one another – which springs, I think, from our fear of our own insignificance, a subset of our dread of mortality – we have of late, we Americans, to our detriment, come to love accolades more than genuine achievement. We have come to see them as the point – and we're happy to compromise standards, or ignore reality, if we suspect that's the quickest way, or only way, to have something to put on the mantelpiece, something to pose with, crow about, something with which to leverage ourselves into a better spot on the social totem pole. No longer is it how you play the game, no longer is it even whether you win or lose, or learn or grow, or enjoy yourself doing it... Now it's "So what does this get me?" As a consequence we cheapen worthy endeavors, and building a Guatemalan medical clinic becomes more about the application to Bowdoin than the well-being of Guatemalans. It's an epidemic – and in its way, not even dear old Wellesley High School... where good is no longer good enough, where a B is the new C, and the midlevel curriculum is called Advanced College Placement. And I hope you caught me when I said "one of the best." I said "one of the best" so we can feel better about ourselves, so we can bask in a little easy distinction, however vague and unverifiable, and count ourselves among the elite, whoever they might be, and enjoy a perceived leg up on the perceived competition. But the phrase defies logic. By definition there can be only one best. You're it or you're not.

If you've learned anything in your years here, I hope it's that education should be for, rather than material advantage, the exhilaration of learning. You've learned, too, I hope, as Sophocles assured us, that wisdom is the chief element of happiness. (Second is ice cream...just an fyi) I also hope you've learned enough to recognize how little you know...how little you know now...at the moment...for today is just the beginning. It's where you go from here that matters.

As you commence, then, and before you scatter to the winds, I urge you to do whatever you do for no reason other than you love it and believe in its importance. Don't bother with work you don't believe in any more than you would a spouse you're not crazy about, lest you too find yourself on the wrong side of a Baltimore Orioles comparison. Resist the easy comforts of complacency, the specious glitter of materialism, the narcotic paralysis of self-satisfaction. Be worthy of your advantages. And read... read all the time... read as a matter of principle, as a matter of self-respect. Read as a nourishing staple of life. Develop and protect a moral sensibility and demonstrate the character to apply it. Dream big. Work hard. Think for yourself. Love everything you love, everyone you love, with all your might. And do so, please, with a sense of urgency, for every tick of the clock subtracts from fewer and fewer; and as surely as there are commencements there are cessations, and you'll be in no condition to enjoy the ceremony attendant to that eventuality no matter how delightful the afternoon.

The fulfilling life, the distinctive life, the relevant life, is an achievement, not something that will fall into your lap because you're a nice person or mommy ordered it from the caterer. You'll note the founding fathers took pains to secure your inalienable right to life, liberty and the pursuit of happiness – quite an active verb, "pursuit" – which leaves, I should think, little time for lying around watching parrots roller-skate on YouTube. The first President Roosevelt, the old rough rider, advocated the strenuous life, Mr. Thoreau wanted to drive life into a corner, to live deep and suck out all the marrow. The poet Mary Oliver tells us to row, row into the swirl and roil. Locally, someone... I forget who...from time to time encourages young scholars to carpe the heck out of the diem. The point is the same: get busy, have at it. Don't wait for inspiration or passion to find you. Get up, get out, explore, find it yourself, and grab hold with both hands. (Now, before you dash off and get your YOLO tattoo, let me point out the illogic of that trendy little expression – because you can and should live not merely once, but every day of your life. Rather than You Only Live Once, it should be You Live Only Once...but because YLOO doesn't have the same ring, we shrug and decide it doesn't matter.)

None of this day-seizing, though, this YLOOing, should be interpreted as license for self-indulgence. Like accolades ought to be, the fulfilled life is a consequence, a gratifying byproduct. It's what happens when you're thinking about more important things. Climb the mountain not to plant your flag, but to embrace the challenge, enjoy the air and behold the view. Climb it so you can see the world, not so the world can see you. Go to Paris to be in Paris, not to cross it off your list and congratulate yourself for being worldly. Exercise free will and creative, independent thought not for the satisfaction they will bring you, but for the good they will do others, the rest of the 6.8 billion – and those who will follow them. And then you too will discover the great and curious truth of human experience is that selflessness is the best thing you can do for yourself. The sweetest joys of life, then, come only with the recognition that you're not special.

Because everyone is.

APPENDIX B

A Special Kind of Stupid: The Persecution of an American Educator

The Left has long used the education system as the microcosm for society, as a whole. It was the original template.

The guerrilla tactics employed by Democrats to take down President Donald Trump, eventually evolved into a blatant, frontal assault on our freedoms and our democracy, through the nullification of 63 million Americans who voted for this President in 2016.

Before the war was declared on President Trump, conservative educators were in the trenches fighting against destructive liberal policies for the minds of our children. They were fighting for American principles, they were fighting for their rights, they were fighting for their jobs and they were fighting for their lives.

This is the story of Robert Sneider, who earned two masters and a doctorate, was an instructor for the Globe Science initiative and a historian for Teaching America's Story, all accomplished in 6 years as a special educator in a Title I school for the New York City Department of Education. This is his story of a conservative educator trying to survive in a corrupted liberal education system.

Preview of A Special Kind of Stupid: The Persecution of an American Educator (rough draft)

It was an unusually steamy morning in late August 2004 when I found myself staring out into the schoolyard from the third-floor window of a junior high school in the Bronx, New York. The students had assembled for the first day of the school year and were preparing to make their way up to the classrooms. Other than a stint as a practice teacher when I was 19 years old, I had never spent a single minute as an educator. I had spent the last 20 years as an electronic technician in the high-tech industry.

That summer I had quit my job (a job, by the way, which had paid very well and provided job security) against the advice of my friends and co-workers and to the horror of my family and relatives and signed up for the 'New York City Urban Teachers' program. This was a program would assist me in getting all the necessary teaching licenses and certifications and subsidize a Master's degree in special education, in return for teaching two years of special education in an inner-city, title I school. I also had to accept a 50% cut in pay, no job guarantee and relocation to one of the most crowded cities on the planet.

I was in the midst of a career change and this was a fellowship program similar to 'Teach for America', that brought teachers from all over the country to high need areas of education, such as special education, in troubled schools and depressed and poverty-stricken environments. The philosophy of the program was to try to bring teachers from the outside in order to break the cycle of poor quality education, perpetrated by poorly educated students, who would then become future teachers and continue the process by passing on their deficient skills to the next generation of students. It goes without saying that these were difficult jobs under difficult circumstances.

The average teacher who has established themselves with a good job in a good school is not the one willing to trade that, to work in a much harsher environment. So these programs, such as 'Teach for

America' and other fellows programs, were designed to offer incentives for educators to go into these deficient and dysfunctional settings and try to improve the quality of education. That's how a middle-aged, Caucasian man, embarking on a new career, found himself smack in the middle of the Bronx, New York, about to receive his first class ever.

It was a huge risk, to be sure, but it was not my lack of experience that was worrying me at this juncture. As I scanned the schoolyard from my third- floor vantage point, I began to realize that there was something that I had not been prepared for and that no one had bothered to mention to this point. Either they assumed that I knew what I was getting into or they didn't want me to quit before I started. The composition of the students in the schoolyard was 99% African-American and Hispanic. My trepidation was not so much about the skin color of the students but what it represented—a different culture. I knew nothing about the African-American culture, about the Hispanic culture and about the general culture of the inner-city environment. That's when it dawned on me how much of a fish-out-of-water I was.

I was born and had grown up in Canada. I don't know if it was the cold and the snow but there just weren't many black persons in Canada, in those days. The first time I even saw a black person in the flesh was when I crossed over the border into Niagara Falls, New York with my friends, when I was fifteen years old, to do some underage imbibing. A few years later, I went to college in an upscale enclave of Massachusetts where really the only persons of color were on scholarship to the basketball team. Years later, I would buy a home in New Hampshire which is arguably one of the whitest states in the union. One time a teacher who had grown up in the diverse environment of New York City visited me and was astounded at how homogenous the population was. It was the truth. I remember being at Hampton beach on a sweltering Fourth of July with a hundred thousand beachgoers and you would have a hard time finding a person of color. The point I am trying to illustrate, is that when it came to the subject of diversity, I had led a very sheltered life

Now not only was I being exposed to diversity in the extreme (for the first time in my life I was a minority in the most dramatic sense) but I was expected to teach these students. Teach them...I had no understanding of what they were about. I had always been under the impression that in order to teach something, you had to have an understanding of your subject and your audience. I certainly had no understanding of my audience. By the way, in case I haven't mentioned it, I had been hired to teach science--a subject for which I had no license or certification. It was a content area in which I had not taken a course since high school some 30 years ago-- but apparently it was a situation in which the New York City Department of Education, in its infinite wisdom, deemed me eminently qualified.

Whatever confidence I had that I could handle the situation, was quickly eroding. My concern was turning to abject fear. I felt the walls closing in on me while the floor (and my life) was collapsing under my feet. I have to confess that I had thoughts of running for the nearest exit--that this was all a big mistake and that I needed to go back to my nice safe life.

"Who needs THIS" I asked myself.
"Not me" I answered myself.

You know you're in real trouble when you find yourself engaged in a two-way conversation, but you are the only one in the room. I was at one of those crucial crossroads in life where the next decision you make will likely determine how the rest of your life goes. Looking back, this was certainly borne out. Then I thought, why was I doing this in the first place? I was doing it because I felt I was at a time in my life when I needed to give something back to others. I had done the private sector thing in pursuit of a paycheck and all its materialism and found it to be lacking. There was something missing in my life. I was restless. I was searching for more purpose. So maybe in the end I did need this. And maybe--just maybe-- they needed what I had to offer. I would never know if I walked out now and the only way I was going to find out is if I stuck around, so I guess in the end it was my curiosity that got the best of me. And culture shock, be damned. Besides, if you view life as a journey then this was just another adventure along the path, and sometimes it's not always about what you learn about the world around you, but what you learn about yourself. After all, one of the tenets of my upbringing was that strength and character was bred from conquering adversity.

What happened next became the template for the rest of the time that I would spend in the Bronx. I became the student. The students would teach me. They would teach me their culture. I had heard that old teacher's saw that "The kids teach me as much as I teach them" and I never really understood what that meant. In the end, they taught me enough to enable me to write this book. Without them, this book would not have been possible and to them this book is dedicated.

The bell rang and the students were on their way up to the classrooms. Having made the decision to stay and see it through, I didn't have much time.

I tried to focus on the task at hand. My immediate concern was how should I greet the student? Should I stand in my doorway as they entered, or should I be seated at my desk? We had been taught in our training that standing at the doorway presented a more authoritarian presence, in which you controlled the situation right from the get-go. However, I opted for the more casual presentation of being seated at my desk, as I hoped that this would be more informal and put the students more at ease. This also had the advantage of hiding my knees, which were knocking pretty badly at this point in the proceedings.

I was soon in for a rude awakening. The first student through my door was a huge kid, at least 6 foot tall and African-American and I thought to myself, *this is an eighth grader…it's a good thing I didn't sign up for high school… what are they feeding these kids nowadays, anyway?* He walked right over to the front of my desk and placed his hands on my desk, looked me straight in the eye and proclaimed "I hate school, I hate teachers and I'm not going to do a F… ing thing you tell me to do." I had already programmed myself into asking the obligatory,

"How was your summer vacation?" which I blurted out right on cue, just as I had rehearsed it and in juxtaposition to what he had just declared, this seemed awkwardly incongruent. This only evoked a look of condescension and he spat out "It sucked and what's it to you anyway?" as he made his way to his seat. First rule a teacher should learn—listen to what your students are telling you. And so it began.

It was in this manner that my teaching career was launched, and I had walked through the door into a whole new world. I will make this comment on my initiation--this would later be verified as we progressed through the school year--that this student, who I will call Alan was true to his word and even made good on things he had not enunciated. He despised school and teachers and operated pretty much on his own schedule, with little fear of school-dispensed repercussions. However, I came to appreciate Alan and his style, whether you liked him or not, because at least he was upfront with you. There were others who were much more insidious with their intentions but as I had said, I had more pressing problems to deal with.

Least of which was that I had no textbooks or course materials. Another situation in which the NYCDOE didn't seem overly concerned about. In fact, there was not a stitch of instructive material in the entire classroom including the walls and shelves of this third-floor hothouse. There I was on the third floor of a brick building that had no air conditioning save for an ancient electric fan in the corner that looked like it was a refugee from the forties. I soon learned that the way to calculate the temperature in your room was to take the outside temperature and add 10° for each floor that you went up. So, for instance if it was 80° outside, the second floor would be 90 and the third floor would be 100°-- especially in afternoons when the sun came through our windows and baked us like worms under a magnifying glass.

I was quickly beginning to see why so many teachers washed out in the first few years of this profession. It's no wonder that in this kind of brutal environment 50% of teachers quit during their first year in teaching, 75% are gone by second year and by the fifth year only 10%

of teachers remain in the profession. It seemed that the approach of the school and the DOE was to provide new teachers with the worst possible conditions and see who survived. It was almost a designed trial by fire. I personally don't agree with this approach, whether by design or accident and I think the system would be better served by providing more support to new teachers but strange as it may seem, this strategy actually worked with me and it made me a better teacher today. At the time, though, I was doing anything I could just to survive. Even the janitors had a betting pool against how long I would last, and the long end bet had me out by the end of the week. Even I had to concede the overly optimistic folly of that wager.

There's an old adage that sailor' recite when they are caught in a storm and the ship is in extreme peril, that I found applied to this situation perfectly. They talk about when 'the waves turn the minutes to hours.' That had to be the longest week of my life. Every time I looked at the clock it seemed to be running backward. Imagine yourself in front of 35 minority kids whose culture you didn't understand, who had no use for education and didn't want to be there, in a room that was 100 degrees, with no educational materials of any kind. I did everything I could think of—told stories, asked questions, led the class in physical exercises, brought in newspapers for current events. One day we found an ancient computer, in pieces, in one of the closets.

This might have been the first computer that Adam and Eve ever used but I didn't care. My previous background was in high-tech and I knew a little bit about hardware and software and so the class project became to put this computer back together. At that point I didn't care if it worked or not--just trying to put it back together would be enough to keep the class occupied, at least for a while and after all this was science class. The bonus was, to the astonishment of all of us, was that once we had it assembled, it not only worked but the printer printed. And aside from computers in the administrative offices, we had the only other working computer in the entire school.

I never knew at the time what a boon this would prove to be for my situation. There was nothing that these kids, poor as they were, related to more than technology. When you came right down to it, they were actually quite computer savvy and so not only could we use the computer for researching and learning about content, but it was a great incentive for them to be granted the privilege to go on it, when they had completed their regular lessons . It was nothing less than a Godsend and it literally saved my teaching career. I learned early on how technology could be incorporated into the classroom and if used properly, what a tool it could be to enhance student engagement and academic performance. That was a lifesaver and I had my technical expertise in my previous life to thank for it. That's how I survived my first week.

One of the Department of Education policies or practices New York was to separate disruptive learners. The philosophy behind this diffusion was one of divide and conquer. There are many students in the inner-city school system that come to school only because the state law requires them to attend until they are 16 years old.

However, these students have no interest in school or learning and are there solely to be as disruptive as possible--derailing education for everyone. For some reason school administrations feel it is more prudent to disperse these problematic students over many classes rather than concentrate them in one or two areas. The theory was that a couple of disruptive students could be more readily managed if they were diluted within a classroom, of say 30 kids, who were more disposed to learning. It was even felt that the majority of learners might provide a positive peer influence for the disruptors to conform. As good as it looked on paper, the opposite happened. In most cases, it only took one or two disruptors to destroy the learning atmosphere for the rest of the students in the classroom.

If you ask any teacher, it only takes one or two disruptive students to render the learning process almost impossible for the other students in the class. I have never understood why the school system feels it is necessary to sacrifice the education of 98% of their students while catering to the 2%. Administration's reluctance to remove these students is dangerous in that it undermines the teacher's authority and it allows an aggressive situation to fester inside the classroom. The kind of behavior exhibited by these students would not be tolerated in any other area of life--at home their parents would punish them, in the street they would be beaten up or arrested and on the job they would be fired--only in the schools does the system empower them to act with virtual impunity.

In my opinion, it came down to a simple case of math. Let's say you had 10 classes of 35 students each and 10 of the 350 were disruptive students. According to the practice of diffusion, one disruptive student would be assigned to each class. If it didn't work and all 10 students continued their disruptive behavior it could have a potential detrimental impact on 350 students. If you grouped all the disruptive students in one class—it allowed 340 to get their education and let's say by some miracle the teacher of the 10 disruptive students was able to reach 3 the ratio of successful learning is 343/350. In anyone's logic, this was a much better ratio although I can't imagine it would have been very enjoyable for the teacher who had the one class from hell.

However, in a world of inclusion, no child left behind, and non-discrimination administrations are often reluctant to adopt the logical situation and this was always one reason why the learning process was undermined in an inner-city environment.

In the course of MY education. I witnessed and learned many things about the culture of this new world that I had entered. And many of these things had more to do with the culture of poverty in the inner-city. There were two incidents in particular that illustrated what a neophyte I was, when it came to the culture that I was now immersed. As I had stated, my class was composed of minorities— African Americans and Hispanics but all were of a dark skin color so that to my untrained and naïve eye it was difficult to distinguish one group from the other. As I was calling on students who had raised their hands, one student asked me why I was such a racist. I was taken aback. I had always thought that the term racist applied to a white and black situation. There were no white kids that I was favoring over any of the black kids because there were no white kids, period. I asked him to explain. "You keep calling on the Hispanics over us African Americans." I was blown away.

Because I had limited exposure to minorities, I was not able to distinguish such subtle differences but obviously there were vast differences to those concerned. I was being schooled in one of the more unattractive traits of human nature. I soon began to realize the culture in these inner-city schools is one of divisiveness. No matter how similar people appear to be, they will strive to find the differences that set them apart. Because once they have defined the differences, they can exploit those to put down other people in order to build themselves up. This is a practice that has been going on since the beginning of time. I remember one student being teased ruthlessly because his parents had bought him the wrong brand of sneakers.

I can honestly say that in my time as a teacher in this environment skin color was never an issue. You quickly become color blind and your only concern becomes who exhibits good behavior and who exhibits bad behavior. I can say that even in this environment there were students who had been instilled with values and morals that I would have hoped to have fostered in my own kids and that was a real credit to the parents who had raised them. In this place, it was like trying to grow a rose between the cracks of a sidewalk.

Another time, I was teaching a class of 8th graders who just happened to consist of all boys. After the lesson, we were having some cooperative time when one of the students asked for permission to play a radio. It was granted. During these times, there is usually a high level of discussion. I was doing some work at my desk when I noticed that it was unusually silent, except for a song that was lightly playing in the background. This was a group of especially tough kids—kids who wouldn't cry if they were cut with a knife and I noticed that many were sobbing to themselves. I asked the student sitting closest to me what was going on. He said that there was a rap song playing with the theme of "I never knew my father" or something to that extent. I still didn't get it, "So?"

"So", he explained, "None of us knew our fathers". You could have knocked me over with a feather. I had no concept of how pervasive the deterioration of the family was in the inner city, until that moment. Twenty kids and not one had a relationship with their natural father. Amazing. It was then that I realized I had no idea of what these kids went through or what their life was like when they left school.

These students also had a strange ritual of fighting in the classroom. This was something that I had never witnessed in all my years of being student. I never saw two students have a physical fight in the classroom. This was a totally new phenomenon--in my day there were fights but these occurred after school or off school property, but never inside a classroom. The fights in the Bronx would often be preceded by another strange ritual of this jungle mentality and survival of the fittest regimen. In fact, it was almost as if it was a behavior learned from animals.

I had observed that many altercations were preceded by verbal sparring, that might include insults and name-calling. In many instances, this escalated into a physical confrontation in which the two students would come together, get into each other's face and butt shoulders, almost like two rams butting heads or horns. At this point, the confrontation could evolve into blows being thrown but I had also seen that the situation could defuse and both students could take their seats. It was as if they had proven that they were not afraid of each other and that they had a mutual respect for each other's courage. Apparently in the code of this jungle, there was no need to prove themselves further. You can find similar instances in nature when two animals confront each other and one submits and further physical domination is avoided.

Physical confrontation is a trait of both a crowded inner-city environment and poverty. Sometimes words are not enough to survive and one must take what one needs by physical force. Physical violence was an everyday concern in my time spent in the Bronx. Fights in the hallways produced a hurricane effect. The hallways at this school were very narrow to begin with and when you packed 1500 students (which by the way was the largest school I had ever been in until I got to college) into them they got even smaller. For some reason, many fights in the hallway started at lunch time and during the return to class a fight might start at the head of the hallway. You would then witness the hurricane effect, as it inevitably seemed to spin its way down the hall, constricted by the sheer number of students packed into a limited space.

Students were pushed aside and they in turn appeared to propel the perpetrators down the corridor. If there was an open classroom door, students were flung into that open space, It was really a phenomenon of physics, that I had never seen before. Another analogy is that of a rat being swallowed whole by a snake and watching the bulge making its way down the digestive track.

The classroom fight could be triggered by one student just looking at someone the wrong way. This produced an atmosphere of tension and always being on the edge. It was a cloud that always hung over our heads and you never knew when it was going to rain. The classroom fight could be a devastating event. Desks and other objects could be thrown around and innocent bystanders could be hurt in the melee. Often, other students were screaming and running out of the room and needless to say the lesson would be totally disrupted. Even once the perpetrators were removed, it would take time to put the room back in order and many times, even if this was accomplished it was almost impossible to get the students back to concentrating on the lesson at hand.

A classroom fight could have other devastating consequences. I certainly didn't escape the experience unscathed. I remember one hot day where the heat was also bringing tempers to the boiling point. We had an ancient relic of a fan that did its best to try and combat the heat but it was a losing battle, even for this ancient warrior.

It was a heavy, steel, floor model with a metal stand and metal blades and a metal protective cage. Suddenly two students exploded into a fight. After having exhorted them to refrain I got on the school's phone near the classroom door to call security, as was the school policy. In the meantime, one of the students actually picked up the spinning fan and tried to hit the other student over the head with it. He missed and the fan cage slammed into a desk. Apparently, the cage was a two-piece assembly and the front part fell off from the impact, leaving the spinning metal blades exposed. This didn't stop the student from trying to jam the fan blades into the face of the other student. When the others in the class saw the intended action, some of them ran out of the room screaming. I was on the phone, with my back turned to the class when one of the students slammed into me accidentally. I was hit full force from behind. My head snapped backward and I saw a spectrum of colors in one of my eyes, then it went black. I thought I had suffered some kind of temporary concussion from the impact, as there was no pain or any sign of injury associated with it, so for the time being I was concerned with more pressing matters. Such as the possible beheading of the student in my classroom. In the end, the only thing that saved the other student was that he had drifted far enough away from the wall plug so that the fan cord came out of the wall socket. Then security came and mopped up.

I went to the hospital to find out that I had suffered a detached retina in my left eye and was told at the time, that it was unlikely that I would ever see again as well as I had. Luckily for me, that initial diagnosis was proven wrong but only after six hours of surgery, two other procedures, months of rehabilitation, the insertion of a plastic lens, all done at New York Presbyterian Hospital, one of the best in the world at this kind of surgery, by the grace of God and a $30,000 hospital bill.

One of the most valuable lessons I ever learned from this atmosphere of always living on the edge of the next physical explosion, was that if you were to survive as a teacher, you had to show no fear. And it gets even gloomier than that. This was an atmosphere of constant threats, gangs, students threatening to commit suicide by jumping from third floor stairwells, fires being set in the school, students being subdued only with straitjackets and medication, physical altercations on a daily basis, not only student on student but student on teacher. Of rolling metal detectors, turning out guns and knives, and yet remarkably no one had actually been killed within the school building (there had been some killings on the streets and neighborhoods surrounding school). It was a running joke among the teachers that in order to get a permanent metal detector installed that, someone had to die within the confines of the school and that we needed a teacher to step up and volunteer themselves, so that our school could qualify. Oddly enough, there were no takers but all joking aside, this was an environment that was not to be taken lightly, in terms of life and death.

I know this is a terrible thing to say in this day and age but there's still a tremendous amount of racial hatred in this country. And what was even more surprising, is that it is so pervasive at such a young age. Students in the sixth and seventh grade have been taught by their parents to hate white people and this goes back several generations. I found myself in a situation where I had to be constantly wary, because in many instances, I was the only white person for miles around. The hatred I felt was palpable and undeniable. I was called every name imaginable, but I guess after a while, people can be conditioned to get used to anything.

I know this may sound like an overreaction to some people, but I literally had to confront the fact there was a possibility that I might actually die doing this job. I know it sounds crazy but until I actually acknowledged that realization I was operating under an atmosphere of constant fear. And I can tell you this, that if these students had even got a whiff that I was the least bit afraid, my teaching career would have been over in that instant--because they would've walked all over me. And in order to get into this state you almost had to pretend that you were like a soldier going into battle and accept the fact that you are going to get killed. Once you accepted that fact, the fear left you and you were actually able to function more effectively. I call this my dead man walking mentality.

When I think back of all the years that I spent in this world of violence and intimidation and with all the threats that were directed at me, I can say that once I accepted the fact that I might die on this job, I can truly say that I was never afraid of any of my students, with the exception of one. In all those years, there were many students who were much larger physically than I was, there were many that were on medications that would make them act irrationally, there were many

214

that were on drugs, there were many that were operating on hate and anger.

Once I had made the determination that, while New York was a great place to visit in terms of resources, such as world class museums and the like, it was not really a place where I would feel comfortable living--it was only a matter of time before I returned to New Hampshire. That time finally came in the summer of 2010 when I was hired to teach in a small school in the White Mountains of northern New Hampshire. Before I left New York, there was one last thing I wanted to do and that was to go to the top of the Empire State Building. It was an incredible experience--one that I will never forget. It was the most dramatic manifestation of the creativity and industry of man that I had ever encountered and that view is forever etched on the canvas of my mind. A week later I was back in New Hampshire and one of the first things I wanted to do—something I had never done—was to climb a mountain. I did so just as the leaves were changing color and I felt like I was standing on the top of the world-- only this was a natural world of indescribable serenity, sculpted by the hand of God.

Within weeks, I had gone from one extreme to the other. The contrast between the two environments could not have been more drastic and yet my studies of school behavior had led me to one undeniable certainty. The probability of encountering an incidence of extreme school violence was just as likely in one place as it was in the other. The rest of this book is dedicated to explaining how that determination is possible.

Printed in the United States
By Bookmasters